READING/WRITING COMPANION

Arianna

Mc Graw Hill Education

Cover: Nathan Love, Erwin Madrid

mheducation.com/prek-12

Send all inquiries to:
McGraw-Hill Education
Two Penn Plaza
New York, NY 10121

ISBN: 978-0-07-901824-3
MHID: 0-07-901824-6

Printed in the United States of America.

5 6 7 8 9 LMN 23 22 21 20   D

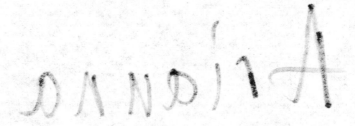

Welcome to Wonders!

Read exciting **Literature**, **Science**, and **Social Studies** texts!

★ LEARN about the world around you!

★ THINK, SPEAK, and WRITE about genres!

★ COLLABORATE in discussion and inquiry!

★ EXPRESS yourself!

my.mheducation.com
Use your student login to read core texts, practice grammar and spelling, explore research projects and more!

GENRE STUDY 1 **EXPOSITORY TEXT**

GENRE STUDY 2 **FOLKTALE**

GENRE STUDY 3 EXPOSITORY TEXT

WRAP UP THE UNIT

 Digital Tools Find this eBook and other resources at **my.mheducation.com**

UNIT 4

GENRE STUDY 1 REALISTIC FICTION

GENRE STUDY 2 EXPOSITORY TEXT

(fox)Jimkruger/iStock/Getty Images;(two)McGraw-Hill Education

GENRE STUDY **3 POETRY**

WRAP UP THE UNIT

 Digital Tools Find this eBook and other resources at **my.mheducation.com**

Talk About It

Astronomers first learned about Earth and our solar system by looking up. Today, scientists use telescopes, satellites, and manned spaceships to study the universe. They make new discoveries every day.

Look at the photo. Look at your partner and listen closely. Ask questions about the discoveries. Write three things you see in the sky.

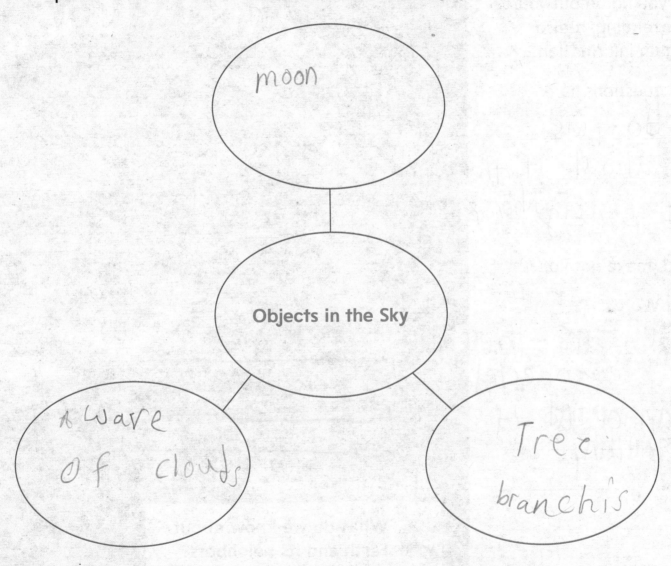

moon

Objects in the Sky

a wave of clouds

Tree branchis

 Go online to **my.mheducation.com**. Read the "Eyes in the Sky" Blast. Think about what we learn from satellites. Blast back your response.

TAKE NOTES

Asking questions before you read helps you figure out your purpose for reading. It also helps you gain information.

Write your questions here.

What do we
know about Earth
and it's neighbors?

As you read, make note of:

Interesting Words:

_____

_____

Key Details: _____

_____

_____

_____

_____

Earth and its neighbors

Essential Question

What do we know about Earth and its neighbors?

Read about how we have learned about space.

Galileo studied the sky with a telescope he built.

Sarin Images/The Granger Collection, NYC

If the Sun could talk, it might say, "Look at me! Look at my sunspots! I am so hot!" Without the Sun, Earth would be a cold, dark planet. How do we know this?

Thanks to the astronomer Galileo, we know a lot about the Sun and the rest of our **solar system**.

Telescopes: Looking Up

Galileo did not invent the telescope. However, 400 years ago he did build one that was strong enough to study the sky. When Galileo looked into space, he saw the rocky **surface** of the Moon. When he looked at the Sun, he discovered spots on its fiery surface.

The Moon is Earth's closest neighbor.

FIND TEXT EVIDENCE 🔍

Read

Paragraphs 1-2
Summarize
What did Galileo study?

Solar system.

Circle text evidence.

Paragraph 3
Main Idea and Key Details
Underline details that describe what Galileo saw. What is the main idea of this section?

Galileo look at the sky with a telescope.

Reread

Author's Craft

How does the author help you see what an astronomer does?

Fluency

Take turns reading the first paragraph with expression. Talk about how the exclamation marks help add feeling.

(tkgd) Ian McKinnell/Photographer's Choice/Getty Images; (b) StockTrek/Photodisc/Getty Images

FIND TEXT EVIDENCE 🔍

Read

Paragraph 1

Key Words

Circle the key word. What does it mean?

Study space.

Paragraphs 2-4

Main Idea and Key Details
Underline important details about satellites. What is the main idea of this section?

Satellites help
scientiests collected
large amount of
information.

Reread

Author's Craft

How does the author help you understand what satellites do?

Astronomy, or the study of space, began with the simple telescope. But astronomers wanted to look at the sky more closely. They made bigger telescopes that could see farther than the one Galileo used. Astronomers still had many questions.

Satellites: A Step Closer

In 1958, scientists launched Explorer 1, the first American satellite, into space. It was an exciting day for America.

Explorer 1 takes off.

Soon many satellites circled the **globe** and took photographs of Earth, the Moon, stars, and other planets. They collected a large **amount** of information. Satellites even tracked the **temperature** on the planet Saturn.

Scientists have learned many things about the solar system from satellites. That's why they kept sending more into space. Soon there were hundreds of satellites in space making amazing discoveries, but astronomers wanted to know even more. That's why they found a way to put a man on the Moon.

(bkgd) NASA, ESA, R. O'Connell (University of Virginia), and the Hubble Heritage Team (STScI/AURA); (c) NASA Marshall Space Flight Center (NASA-MSFC)

One Giant Leap

On April 12, 1961, Russian cosmonaut Yury Gagarin became the first man to travel into space. Just 23 days later, American **astronaut** Alan Shepard followed. Both flights were short, but they proved that people could go into space.

After Shepard, more astronauts went into space. Some orbited Earth. Some walked on the dusty, bumpy **surface** of the Moon. They took pictures and collected Moon rocks. Astronauts wanted to answer some important questions. Did the Sun's **warmth** heat the Moon? Could the Moon **support** life someday?

Astronaut Edwin "Buzz" Aldrin walks toward the lunar module. Aldrin left his footprints on the Moon.

Aldrin brought home this Moon rock.

(l) MPI/Archive Photos/Getty Images; (r) NASA-JSC

FIND TEXT EVIDENCE

Read

Paragraph 1

Summarize

Why was 1961 an important year for space exploration? Summarize in your own words.

In 1961 two Poeple went to space. This prowd that it was Possiblie.

Underline text evidence.

Paragraph 2

Suffixes

Circle two words that describe the surface of the Moon. Write what they mean here.

dusty and bumpy Surface.

Reread

Author's Craft

Why is "One Giant Leap" a good heading for this section?

SHARED READ

Read

Paragraph 1

Summarize

Draw a box around details that show what scientists did. Summarize in your own words.

Scientists studied the photographs and moon rocks that the astronauts brought back.

Paragraph 2

Main Idea and Key Details

Underline key details that tell you about the Hubble Space Telescope. What is the main idea of this section?

Studing the solar system and greting close-ups.

Scientists studied the photographs and Moon rocks that the astronauts brought back. They made exciting discoveries using telescopes and satellites. But it wasn't enough. Scientists wanted to get closer to the other planets. Soon they found a way!

Hubble and Beyond

Scientists created another telescope, but this time it was gigantic. They sent it up into space. The Hubble Space Telescope was launched in 1990. It's still up there and orbits Earth above the clouds. It takes clear, close-up photographs of stars and planets. It sends fascinating information back to Earth. The Hubble helps scientists study Earth and its neighbors. It also helps astronomers see planets outside our solar system.

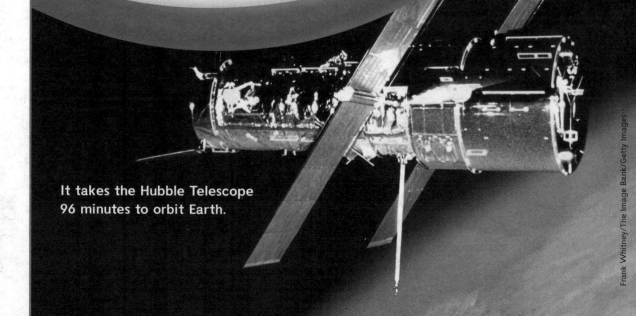

It takes the Hubble Telescope 96 minutes to orbit Earth.

Frank Whitney/The Image Bank/Getty Images

More Discoveries Every Day

Scientists are still asking questions about Earth and its neighbors in space. With the help of satellites, telescopes, and astronauts, they will continue to **explore** and find answers.

What Can We See?

With Our Eyes	With a Simple Telescope	With the Hubble Telescope
The Moon	Craters on the moon	Planets outside our solar system
The Sun	Sunspots	Stars bigger than the Sun and farther away
Mars	Clouds around Jupiter	Jupiter's surface

This is a Hubble Telescope photo of an exploding star.

Summarize

Use your notes to summarize the important details and ideas in "Earth and Its Neighbors."

FIND TEXT EVIDENCE

Read

Paragraph 1

Key Words

Circle the word *explore*. Write an important detail about it.

find awnsers

_____

Page 7

Charts

Underline three things you can see with the Hubble Telescope.

List three things you can see with your eyes.

Planets outside our
Solar System stars
bigger than the sun and far
away Jupiter's surface

Reread

Author's Craft

How does the author use key words to help you understand more about space?

Vocabulary

Use the sentences to talk with a partner about each word. Then answer the questions.

amount

James drank a small **amount** of water.

What could you use to carry a large amount of water?

_____

_____

astronomy

Kia studied **astronomy** to learn more about stars.

What could you learn about by studying astronomy?

_____

_____

globe

Earth is a big, round **globe**.

What is another word for globe?

_____

_____

solar system

Mercury is one of the planets in our **solar system**.

What is at the center of our solar system?

_____

_____

support

My dad and I **support** our favorite baseball team by cheering.

What can you do to show your support?

_____

_____

 Build Your Word List Draw a box around the word *simple* on page 4. In your writer's notebook, use a word web to write words that mean almost the same thing. Use a dictionary to help you.

surface

The **surface** of the Moon is dry and dusty.

Describe the surface of your desk.

_____

_____

temperature

We can have fun even when the **temperature** outside is cold.

What is the temperature where you are today?

_____

_____

warmth

Will and Paul cooked marshmallows over the **warmth** of a fire.

What is another word for warmth?

_____

_____

Suffixes

A suffix is a word part added to the end of a word. It changes the word's meaning. The suffix *-y* means "full of." The suffix *-ly* means "in a certain way."

FIND TEXT EVIDENCE

On page 3 in "Earth and Its Neighbors" I see the word rocky. Rocky *has the suffix -y. I know that the suffix -y means "full of." The word* rocky *must mean "full of rocks."*

When Galileo looked into space, he saw the rocky surface of the Moon.

Your Turn Find the suffix. Use it to figure out the word's meaning.

closely, page 4 _____

_____

Summarize

When you summarize, you state the most important ideas and details in a text. Use these ideas and details to help you summarize "Earth and Its Neighbors."

🔍 FIND TEXT EVIDENCE

How did telescopes help us learn about space? Identify important ideas and details, and summarize them in your own words.

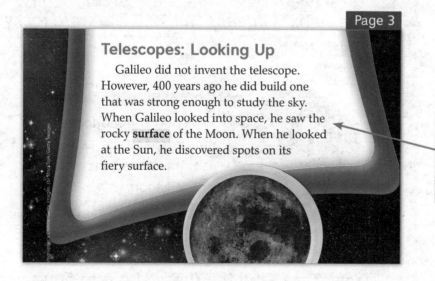

Page 3

Telescopes: Looking Up

   Galileo did not invent the telescope. However, 400 years ago he did build one that was strong enough to study the sky. When Galileo looked into space, he saw the rocky **surface** of the Moon. When he looked at the Sun, he discovered spots on its fiery surface.

I read that Galileo built a telescope. He discovered sunspots and saw the Moon's surface. Details help me summarize. Telescopes helped scientists learn more about space.

Your Turn Reread "Satellites: A Step Closer" on page 4. Think about the most important ideas and details in this section. Then summarize the section here.

_____

_____

Key Words and Charts

"Earth and Its Neighbors" is **expository text**. Expository text

- gives facts and information about a topic
- has text features such as headings, key words, and charts

FIND TEXT EVIDENCE

I can tell that "Earth and Its Neighbors" is an expository text. It gives facts and information about telescopes, satellites, and space. It has headings, key words, and a chart.

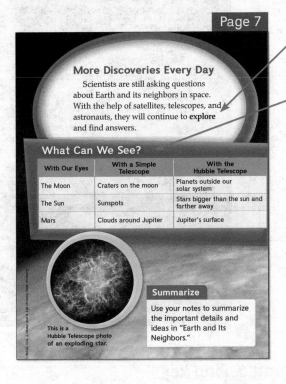

Page 7

More Discoveries Every Day

Scientists are still asking questions about Earth and its neighbors in space. With the help of satellites, telescopes, and astronauts, they will continue to **explore** and find answers.

What Can We See?

With Our Eyes	With a Simple Telescope	With the Hubble Telescope
The Moon	Craters on the moon	Planets outside our solar system
The Sun	Sunspots	Stars bigger than the sun and farther away
Mars	Clouds around Jupiter	Jupiter's surface

Summarize

Use your notes to summarize the important details and ideas in "Earth and Its Neighbors."

This is a Hubble Telescope photo of an exploding star.

Key Words

Key words are important words in the text.

Chart

A chart is a list of facts arranged in rows and columns. It helps readers compare information.

Your Turn Look at the chart on page 7. Write one way the Hubble telescope is different from a simple telescope.

COLLABORATE

_____

_____

_____

Main Idea and Key Details

The main idea is the most important point an author makes about a topic. Key details tell about the main idea.

🔍 **FIND TEXT EVIDENCE**

I can reread the first paragraph on page 4 and look for key details. Then I can think about what these details have in common in order to figure out the main idea.

Main Idea
Astronomers are always searching for new tools that will help them better study space.
Detail
Astronomers wanted to look at the sky more closely.
Detail
They made bigger telescopes that could see farther than the one Galileo used.
Detail
Astronomy, the study of space, began with a simple telescope.

Your Turn Reread "One Giant Leap" on pages 5 and 6. Find key details that tell you about astronauts. List them in your graphic organizer. Use details to figure out the main idea.

Main Idea
Detail
Detail
Detail

Respond to Reading

COLLABORATE

Talk about the prompt below. Think about the print and graphic features in the passage. Use your notes and graphic organizer.

How does the author help you understand more about Earth and its neighbors?

_____

_____

_____

_____

_____

_____

_____

_____

_____

Taking Notes

Plagiarism is copying an author's exact words and using them as your own. As you take notes, avoid plagiarism by **paraphrasing**, or writing information in your own words. Paraphrasing helps you understand a topic better.

Reread this excerpt from "Seeing Red."

> Scientists wanted to know what Mars was once like. They sent machines called rovers to find out.

Now read these two sentences. **Circle** the one that is an example of paraphrasing.

- Scientists wanted to know what Mars was once like so they sent machines called rovers.
- Scientists sent rovers to explore and learn about Mars.

Select a Genre Research the solar system. Use two sources to find interesting information. Then think about how to present the information. Select a genre, for example, a persuasive essay, expository essay, or a poem that matches your topic and audience. Plan a first draft by brainstorming your ideas. Remember to:

- Paraphrase interesting information.
- Create a works cited page, or a list of your sources.
- Make a poster of the solar system. Label the planets.

NASA

Earth

? How do the diagrams and labels help you understand more about the solar system?

COLLABORATE

Talk About It Look at the diagram on pages 198 and 199. Talk with a partner about what the diagram helps you understand.

Cite Text Evidence Why does the author include graphic features, such as the diagram, and print features, such as the heading and caption? Write why in the chart.

Text Feature	How It Helps

Literature Anthology: pages 194–207

Quick Tip

Pay careful attention to text features in an expository text. Headings often state the main idea of a section of text. Captions and diagrams add more information. Use these features to understand the topic better.

Write The author uses text features to help me _____

_____

_____

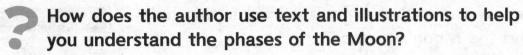

? **How does the author use text and illustrations to help you understand the phases of the Moon?**

COLLABORATE

Talk About It Reread page 204. Talk with a partner about the diagram and what it shows about the phases of the Moon.

Cite Text Evidence How do the clues in the text, diagram, and caption work together to help you understand the Moon's phases? Use the chart to record evidence.

Reread page 204.

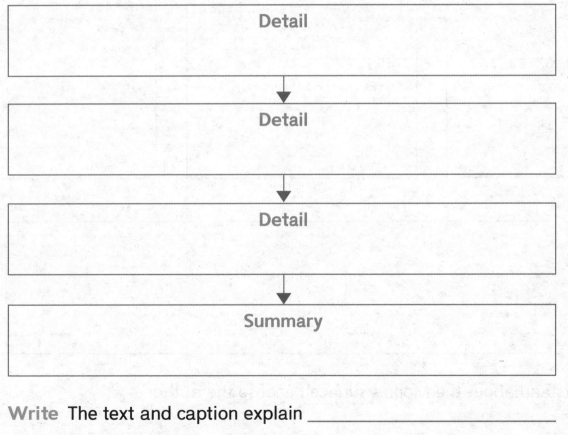

Detail

↓

Detail

↓

Detail

↓

Summary

Write The text and caption explain _____

_____

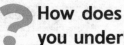

How does the way the author organizes information help you understand the Moon's surface?

Talk About It Reread page 206. Describe to a partner what the surface of the Moon looks like.

Cite Text Evidence How does the author organize the information about the Moon's surface? Write evidence in the chart and explain how it helps you understand the topic.

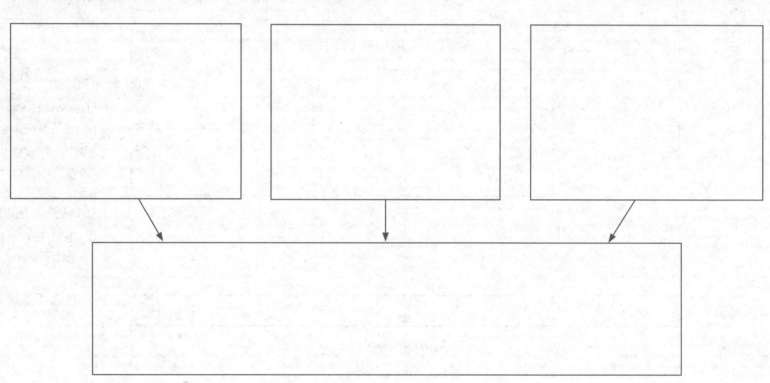

Write I understand about the Moon's surface because the author

_____

_____

Respond to Reading

Answer the prompt below. Think about the text features in the passage. Use your notes and graphic organizer. When you can write a response, you show your understanding of the text.

How does Jefferey Zuehlke use text features to help you learn more about Earth?

_____

_____

_____

_____

_____

_____

_____

_____

_____

Why the Sun Is Red

1   "I'm wondering," said the King to his horseman, while pointing to the rosy sunset. "Why is the Sun red while setting and rising, but yellow the rest of the day?"

2   "Perhaps it's not for us to know," said the horseman.

3   "The Sun's mother must know," said the King. "You're just the one to find her, in her amber house. Its surface glows bright orange. If you find the answer to my question, I'll fill your hat with gold!" said the King. "But if you don't, you must leave my kingdom forever."

4   For seven days the horseman searched. Then, one rainy evening, he saw a glow. It was the amber house! An old woman opened the door. It was the Sun's mother.

Literature Anthology: pages 210–211

Reread and use the prompts to take notes in the text.

Reread paragraphs 1–3. **Underline** the King's question. Write how the horseman will find the answer for the King.

_____

_____

_____

Circle the clues in paragraph 4 that show that the horseman has found the Sun's mother.

COLLABORATE

Reread paragraphs 2–4. Discuss how the horseman feels about being sent to answer the King's question. **Draw a box around** text evidence that helps you understand how the horseman feels.

1   The Sun returned, and the mother said, "A man was here. He wished to know why you're red when you rise and set, but yellow the rest of the day."

2   "How dare he ask!" shouted the Sun.

3   "He left," said her mother. "But why are you angry? It's a simple question."

4   "I'm angry because every morning and evening I draw near the sea and see her," said the Sun.

5   "Her?"

6   "She is the most beautiful princess in the world. She makes me red with envy."

7   The horseman had his answer. He sped away on his horse.

8   The pleased King had his answer. He filled the horseman's hat with gold. The horseman bowed and left quickly, eager for the warmth of his own bed.

Circle evidence in paragraphs 1–6 that shows how the Sun feels. Describe how she feels in your own words.

_____

_____

_____

COLLABORATE

Reread paragraphs 7 and 8. **Underline** phrases that help you visualize what happens after the horseman gives the King his answer. Talk with a partner about how visualizing what he does helps you understand how he feels.

Remember to listen actively to your partner. Ask questions that have to do with understanding how the horseman feels. Make comments that stick to the topic you are discussing.

? **How does the author use third-person point of view to show how the horseman and the Sun feel?**

Talk About It Reread the selections on pages 20 and 21. Discuss what the author does to show how the characters feel.

Cite Text Evidence What text evidence helps you understand how the horseman and the Sun feel?

The Horseman	The Sun

Write I know how the characters feel because the author

_____

_____

Word Choice

Readers to Writers

When you write, repeat a few of the most important points you want to get across in your story. This will help readers notice and remember important details.

Legends are traditional tales that are handed down from generation to generation. They are often told out loud instead of written down. Repeating words and phrases helps the storyteller and the listeners remember the most important parts of the story.

Writers can also repeat words and phrases to help readers notice and remember important details.

FIND TEXT EVIDENCE

On page 20, the King asks a question. Then, later in the legend, the horseman and the Sun's mother repeat the question.

> "Why is the Sun red while setting and rising, but yellow the rest of the day?"

Your Turn Reread paragraph 1 on page 21.

- How does the author's use of repetition help you understand the legend? _____

_____

- Why is "Why the Sun Is Red" a good title for the legend?

_____

_____

Text Connections

? **How is Alexandre Santerne's purpose for creating the photograph similar to why the authors wrote *Earth* and "Why the Sun Is Red"?**

Talk About It Discuss what you see in the photograph. Read the caption and talk about why the stars look like trails.

Cite Text Evidence **Circle** clues in the photograph that help you understand how Earth moves. Then reread the caption and underline how Alexandre Santerne created the photograph.

Write The authors' purposes are like the photographer's purpose

because _____

_____

_____

_____

_____

This photograph is called "Star Trails over La Silla." To create it, photographer Alexandre Santerne took many pictures of the stars at night. Then she combined all of the photos into one. The stars look like trails because of Earth's rotation.

ESO/A. Santerne

Present Your Work

Discuss how you will present your project to the class. Use the Presenting Checklist as you practice reading your information and sharing your poster.

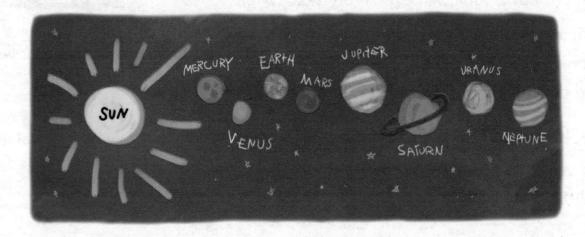

Before presenting, I will fact-check my presentation by_____

_____

I think the information in my presentation was _____

_____

I know because _____

_____

_____

Presenting Checklist

☐ I will make sure I used trusted sources.

☐ I will identify the planets in my poster.

☐ I will speak loudly and clearly enough to communicate ideas effectively.

☐ I will check that my works cited page is in alphabetical order.

Literature Anthology: pages 194-207

Expert Model

Features of an Expository Essay

An expository essay is a form of expository text. It presents ideas and information about a topic. An expository text

- has an introduction that makes the reader want to read more
- presents interesting facts, details, and information
- has a strong conclusion that relates to the topic

Analyze an Expert Model Reread the first paragraph on page 196 of *Earth* in the **Literature Anthology**. Use text evidence to answer the questions.

How does the way the author starts the selection make you want

to read more? _____

_____

_____

What does the author do to make the topic more interesting?

_____

_____

_____

Word Wise

Jeffrey Zuehlke uses proper nouns when writing about a specific person, place, or thing. Proper nouns begin with a capital letter, no matter where they are in a sentence.

Plan: Choose Your Topic

Brainstorm With a partner, brainstorm a list of the planets in our solar system. Use the sentence starters to talk about ideas.

One of the planets in our solar system is . . .

A fact that I know about this planet is . . .

Writing Prompt Choose one of the planets as your topic for an expository essay. Ask yourself what you know about this planet. What is its relationship to the Sun? Is it a gas or a rocky planet? What is special about it?

I will write about _____.

Purpose and Audience An author's purpose is his or her main reason for writing. An audience is who will be reading the work.

The reason I am writing about this planet is

_____

_____

_____

Plan Think about what information you want your readers to know about this planet. In your writer's notebook, draw an Idea web. Write the name of the planet in the middle circle.

Quick Tip

When you write an expository text, you are teaching your audience things you believe they should know about your topic. As you plan your expository text, ask yourself: *What are the most important facts that I want to tell my audience about this planet? What kind of text features would help them understand these facts better?*

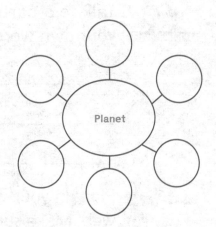

Planet

Plan: Research

Paraphrasing vs. Plagiarism Writers do research to find facts that help them understand their topic. To tell readers where they got the facts, they list their sources on a works cited page. Copying exact words from a source without saying where the words are from is called plagiarism. Plagiarism is like stealing someone else's work.

To avoid plagiarism, you should paraphrase, or put what you learned in your own words.

Read this sentence from "Earth and Its Neighbors."

Satellites even tracked the temperature on the planet Saturn.

Talk to a partner about how you can write about this sentence in your own words. Paraphrase the sentence here.

_____

_____

_____

Plan In your writer's notebook, add important facts to your Idea web. Make sure the facts describe the planet you chose to write about and are paraphrased, or written in your own words.

Quick Tip

You can always have an adult help you come up with your research plan for your expository essay. As you follow your research plan look for relevant information from reliable sources. Check in with an adult if you have any questions about the materials you collect.

Digital Tools

For more information on how to take notes, watch "Take Notes: Print." Go to **my.mheducation.com**.

Draft

Develop Your Topic Writers use facts related to their topic to explain their ideas to readers. They try to choose facts readers might not already know. They use definitions to explain terms readers might not know and interesting details to grab readers' attention. Remember to include enough facts, definitions, and details to help readers understand and be interested in your topic.

Reread page 200 of *Earth* in the **Literature Anthology**. Look for facts and definitions. Look for interesting information. Use text evidence to answer the questions.

What is one interesting fact that you read? Paraphrase it here.

_____

_____

_____

_____

Find one term that has a definition next to it. Write the term and definition here.

_____

_____

Write a Draft Use your Idea web to write your draft in your writer's notebook. Remember to describe facts in your own words.

Revise

Strong Conclusion Writers end an expository essay with a strong conclusion. They summarize the important ideas of the text. They often use an interesting ending to help the reader remember what he or she has learned.

Reread page 207 of *Earth* in the **Literature Anthology**. Talk with a partner about the author's conclusion. Write about it here.

Revise your sentence structure to make your conclusion as clear as possible. Think about combining and rearranging ideas or deleting ideas you don't need.

_____

_____

Revise It's time to revise your writing. Read your draft and look for places where you might

- add more details to support your main ideas

- add a chart or a photograph

- add a strong conclusion or catchy ending

Circle two sentences in your draft that you can change. Revise and write them here.

_____

_____

_____

wavebreakmedia/Shutterstock.com

Peer Conferences

Review a Draft Listen carefully as a partner reads his or her draft aloud. Say what you like about the draft. Use these sentence starters to discuss your partner's draft.

I like this part because it helped me learn . . .

Add another fact to explain . . .

I have a question about . . .

Add a heading, key word, or chart here to . . .

Partner Feedback After you take turns giving each other feedback, write one of the suggestions from your partner that you will use in your revision.

_____

_____

_____

_____

_____

Revision After you finish your peer conference, use the Revising Checklist to figure out what you can change to make your expository essay better. Remember to use the rubric on page 33 to help with your revision.

 Revising Checklist

☐ Did I include details that support the main ideas of my essay?

☐ Did I paraphrase the information that I found in my research?

☐ Does my text end with a strong conclusion?

☐ Did I include helpful headings, key words, or charts?

Tech Tip

If you are writing your draft on a computer, you can easily highlight key words or make headings stand out by making them bold or changing the font.

Edit and Proofread

After you revise your expository text, proofread it to find any mistakes in grammar, spelling, and punctuation. Read your draft at least three times. This will help you catch any mistakes. Use the checklist below to edit your sentences.

Grammar Connections

When you proofread your draft, remember to use a capital letter at the beginning of every proper noun. A proper noun can be the name of a person or a place such as Jupiter or Earth.

✔ Editing Checklist

☐ Do all sentences begin with a capital letter and end with a punctuation mark?

☐ Are all of the sentences complete?

☐ Do the proper nouns begin with capital letters?

☐ Are all the words spelled correctly?

List two mistakes that you found as you proofread your expository text.

1 _____

_____

_____

2 _____

_____

_____

Publish, Present and Evaluate

Publishing When you publish your writing, you create a neat final copy that is free of mistakes. If you are not using a computer, use your best handwriting. Write legibly in print or cursive.

Presentation Practice your presentation. Use the Presenting Checklist.

Evaluate After you publish, use the rubric to evaluate your essay.

What did you do well? _____

_____

What needs some improvement? _____

_____

Presenting Checklist

☐ Look at the audience.

☐ Speak loudly and clearly.

☐ Explain any charts or diagrams included in your essay.

☐ Answer questions thoughtfully.

4	3	2	1
• planet's relation to the Sun is clearly stated • includes many facts and a strong conclusion • all proper nouns are capitalized and spelled correctly	• planet's relation to the Sun is stated • includes some facts and a conclusion • most proper nouns are capitalized and spelled correctly	• planet is stated but not its relation to the Sun • includes a few facts but conclusion might be missing • several capitalization or spelling errors	• planet and its relation to the Sun are unclear • has few facts and no conclusion • many capitalization and spelling errors

? Essential Question

What makes different animals unique?

Bottlenose dolphins are unique mammals. Their shape helps them glide through water. They talk to each other by whistling. All animals have unique qualities. They use their special features to get what they need, protect themselves, and communicate.

Look at the photograph. Talk about other animals with unique qualities. Remember to listen actively. Write your ideas here.

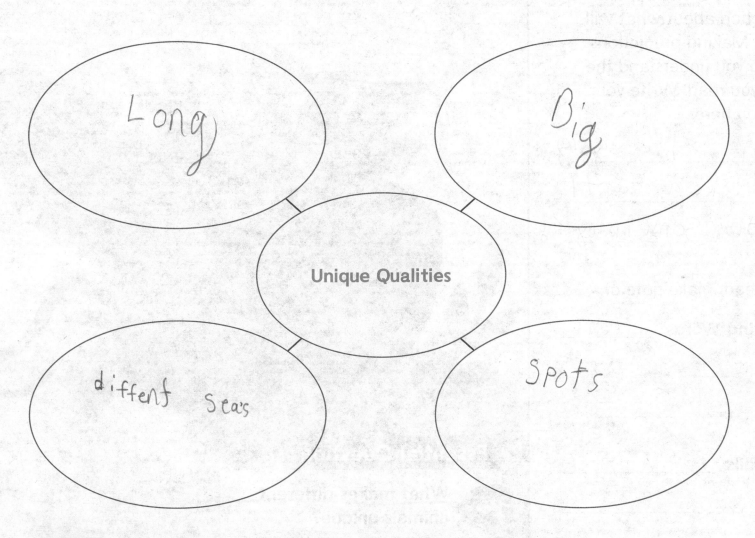

Long

Big

Unique Qualities

diffent Sea's

Spots

BLAST BACK!
studysync

Go online to **my.mheducation.com** and read "The Perfect Predator" Blast. Think about what makes the shark a good hunter. Then blast back your response.

Peter Pinnock/Stockbyte/Getty Images

TAKE NOTES

Look over the illustrations in this passage and think about the title. Then, make a prediction about what will happen. Making predictions can help you understand the text as you read. Write your prediction here.

Anansi is going to trick a turtle or do something bad.

As you read, make note of:

Interesting Words: _____

_____

_____

Key Details: _____

_____

_____

_____

Anansi
Learns a Lesson

Essential Question

?

What makes different animals unique?

Read about how Turtle solves his problem.

Anansi the Spider loved to play tricks on his friends. One afternoon, Turtle stopped by as Anansi was making lunch. 1

"I hate to bother you as you get ready to eat your meal, but those bananas look **splendid**," said the shy Turtle. "I am so hungry." 2

Anansi was careful and kept a **watchful** eye on this food. He didn't want to share his lunch. So he decided to play a trick on Turtle. 3

"Please, help yourself," Anansi said with a sly and tricky grin as he **offered** Turtle some food. 4

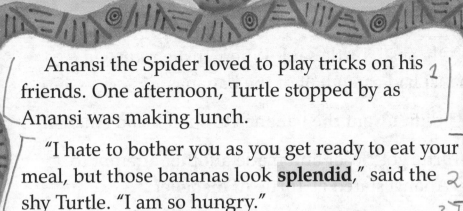

FIND TEXT EVIDENCE

Read

Paragraphs 1–2

Problem and Solution

What is Turtle's problem?

Turtle is so hungry.

Underline the text evidence.

Paragraph 3

Visualize

Draw a box around words or phrases that help you visualize, or picture, what Anansi is like.

Paragraph 4

Synonyms

Circle a synonym for the word *sly*. Write what *sly* means here.

tricky

Reread

Author's Craft

How does the author use dialogue to help you understand what Turtle is like?

FIND TEXT EVIDENCE

Read

Paragraphs 1-5
Visualize
Underline text that helps you picture how Anansi keeps Turtle from eating the bananas.

Paragraphs 6-7
Problem and Solution
What is Turtle's problem?

Turtle didn't get
any bananas.

Draw a box around text that supports your answer.

Illustrations
Circle evidence in the illustration that helps you understand how Turtle feels.

Reread
Author's Craft

How does the author help you understand why Turtle is upset?

Turtle reached for the food. "Aren't you going to wash your hands first?" asked Anansi.

"Oh, yes!" Turtle said. When Turtle returned, Anansi had eaten half of the bananas.

"I didn't want the bananas to spoil," said Anansi.

Turtle got closer and made another attempt to eat. Anansi stared at Turtle in **disbelief**.

"Turtle, please wash your hands, again," he said.

Turtle was upset and filled with **dismay**. He knew his hands were clean, but he went to wash them again. When he returned Anansi had eaten all of the fruit.

"Ha, ha, I tricked you, Turtle," said Anansi. "You didn't get any bananas!"

Turtle was angry that Anansi had tricked him. But he was also tricky and clever. These were two of his best **features**. He decided to play a little trick on his friend. *1*

"Please come to my house at the bottom of the lake for a **fabulous** feast tomorrow," said Turtle. Anansi quickly said yes to the meal. *2*

Turtle decided to ask Fish to help. "Fish, I want to play a little trick on Anansi," he said. "Will you help?" *3*

Fish agreed and together the two friends created a **unique** or one of a kind plan. *4*

FIND TEXT EVIDENCE

Read

Paragraph 1
Problem and Solution
How does Turtle plan to solve his problem?

Turtle is going to trick Anansi.

Circle text evidence.

Paragraph 2
Synonyms
Draw a box around the synonym for *feast*.

Paragraphs 2-4
Make Inferences
Use what Turtle says to make an inference about how he will trick Anansi. Write it here.

turtle is going to invite Anansi to a feast but trick him.

FIND TEXT EVIDENCE

Read

Paragraphs 1–3

Problem and Solution

Why is the lake a problem for Anansi?

Spiters can't swim and can't sink.

How does Fish help him solve his problem? **Circle** Fish's solution.

Paragraph 4

Visualize

Draw a box around text that helps you visualize what Anansi finds at Turtle's house.

Illustrations

Circle two details in the illustration that help you understand the setting.

Reread

Author's Craft

How does the author use repetition to help you understand what *sank* means?

1 The next day, Fish met Anansi at the edge of the lake. "Come Anansi," said Fish. "We will swim to Turtle's house together." Anansi looked at the water. He was an awkward and clumsy swimmer. He was also very light.

2 "How will I ever get down to Turtle's house?" he cried.

3 "Grab some heavy stones," said Fish. "Then you will be heavy enough to sink."

Anansi picked up two big stones, jumped into the lake, and sank down, down, down. At Turtle's house, Anansi saw a wonderful feast of berries.

"Welcome, Anansi," said Turtle. "Drop those stones and help yourself." } 1

As soon as Anansi dropped the stones, he rocketed to the surface of the lake. Anansi sputtered furiously. "Fish and Turtle tricked me," he cried angrily. } 2

Back at the bottom of the lake, Turtle and Fish laughed and laughed. } 3

"Anansi has tricked us many times," said Turtle. "For once, we tricked him." } 4

Summarize

Use your notes and think about what happens in "Anansi Learns a Lesson." Summarize the important events. Talk about whether the prediction you made on page 36 was confirmed.

FIND TEXT EVIDENCE

Read

Paragraphs 1–2

Problem and Solution

What problem does Anansi have when he drops the stones? **Underline** the answer.

Paragraph 2

Visualize

Circle details that help you visualize how Anansi feels. Write how he feels.

angry

Paragraphs 2–4

Lesson

What lesson does Anansi learn?

Not to trick People

Reread

Author's Craft

How does the author help you understand how Turtle and Fish feel about tricking Anansi?

Vocabulary

Use the sentences to talk with a partner about each word. Then answer the questions.

disbelief

Winnie stared in **disbelief** at the huge shark.

What is something that would make you stare in disbelief?

_____

_____

dismay

Marco looked at the rain with sadness and **dismay**.

Describe a time when you felt dismay.

_____

_____

> **Build Your Word List** Reread page 41. Draw a box around interesting words. Choose a word that you noted and look up its meaning. Use print or digital resources.

fabulous

The fireworks were amazing and **fabulous**.

What do you think is fabulous?

_____

_____

features

My kitten's pink nose is one of its cutest **features**.

What is one of your best features?

_____

_____

offered

Jayden **offered** to help Mia pick up her books.

How has someone offered to help you?

_____

_____

splendid

Katie's day at the zoo ended with a wonderful, **splendid** surprise.

List words that mean the same as splendid.

_____

_____

unique

The armadillo's bony armor makes it a **unique** animal.

What is something that makes you unique?

_____

_____

watchful

The ducklings learned to swim under the **watchful** eyes of their mother.

When do you need to be watchful?

_____

_____

Synonyms

Synonyms are words that have the same meaning. Use them as context clues to figure out the meaning of words you don't know.

FIND TEXT EVIDENCE

On page 39, I'm not sure what tricky _means. I see the context clue_ clever _in the same sentence. I know that_ clever _means "smart and skillful" I think_ tricky _and_ clever _are synonyms. They have almost the same meaning. Now I know that_ tricky _means "smart and skillful."_

Turtle was angry that Anansi had tricked him. But he was also tricky and clever.

Your Turn Find a synonym for this word from the folktale.

awkward, page 40 _____

_____

Visualize

Use colorful words and details to help you visualize, or form pictures, in your mind. This will help you understand the characters' actions and feelings.

🔍 **FIND TEXT EVIDENCE**

Look at "Anansi Learns a Lesson" page 38. You might not be sure why Turtle feels upset. Use the details in this part of the story to visualize how he feels.

Page 38

Turtle was upset and filled with **dismay**. He knew his hands were clean, but he went to wash them again. When he returned Anansi had eaten all of the fruit.

I read that Turtle is upset and filled with dismay when he has to wash his hands again. He knows they are already clean. These details help me figure out that Turtle feels confused and frustrated about having to wash his hands a second time.

Your Turn Reread the first two paragraphs on page 41. Why doesn't Anansi eat the berries? Visualize what happens. Then write the answer here.

_____

_____

Illustrations and Lessons

"Anansi Learns a Lesson" is a **folktale**. A folktale

- is a short story passed from parents to children in a culture
- has illustrations that help tell the story
- usually has a message or teaches a lesson

FIND TEXT EVIDENCE

I can tell that "Anansi Learns a Lesson" is a folktale. I learned how Turtle solved a problem he had. I also learned a lesson.

Readers to Writers

Think about the lesson in "Anansi Learns a Lesson." When you write, think about using what characters do and feel to help your readers understand the message of your story.

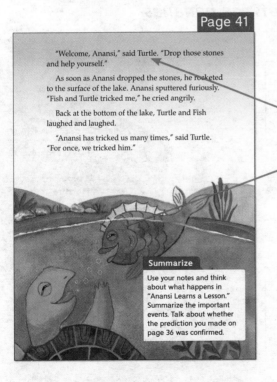

Page 41

"Welcome, Anansi," said Turtle. "Drop those stones and help yourself."

As soon as Anansi dropped the stones, he rocketed to the surface of the lake. Anansi sputtered furiously. "Fish and Turtle tricked me," he cried angrily.

Back at the bottom of the lake, Turtle and Fish laughed and laughed.

"Anansi has tricked us many times," said Turtle. "For once, we tricked him."

Summarize

Use your notes and think about what happens in "Anansi Learns a Lesson." Summarize the important events. Talk about whether the prediction you made on page 36 was confirmed.

Message or Lesson

The message or lesson in a folktale is sometimes found at the end of the story. It is a message the author thinks is important.

Illustrations

Illustrations give more information.

Your Turn Think about the lesson that Anansi learns in "Anansi Learns a Lesson." What message do you think the author is trying to share?

_____

_____

_____

Problem and Solution

A plot is what happens in the beginning, middle, and end of a story. It often has a problem and solution. To follow the plot of a folktale, it helps to pay attention to the problems characters face and how they solve them.

🔍 FIND TEXT EVIDENCE

On pages 37 and 38, I read that Turtle asks Anansi for some bananas. This is a problem for Anansi because he doesn't want to share. Anansi solves this problem by tricking Turtle. He tells Turtle to wash his hands. While Turtle is gone, Anansi eats the bananas. These are steps to solving the problem.

Problem
Anansi doesn't want to share his bananas.

↓

Anansi tricks Turtle into washing his hands.

↓

Anansi eats the bananas.

↓

Solution

 Your Turn Reread pages 39–41 of "Anansi Learns a Lesson." What is Turtle's problem and how does he solve it? List the steps in the graphic organizer.

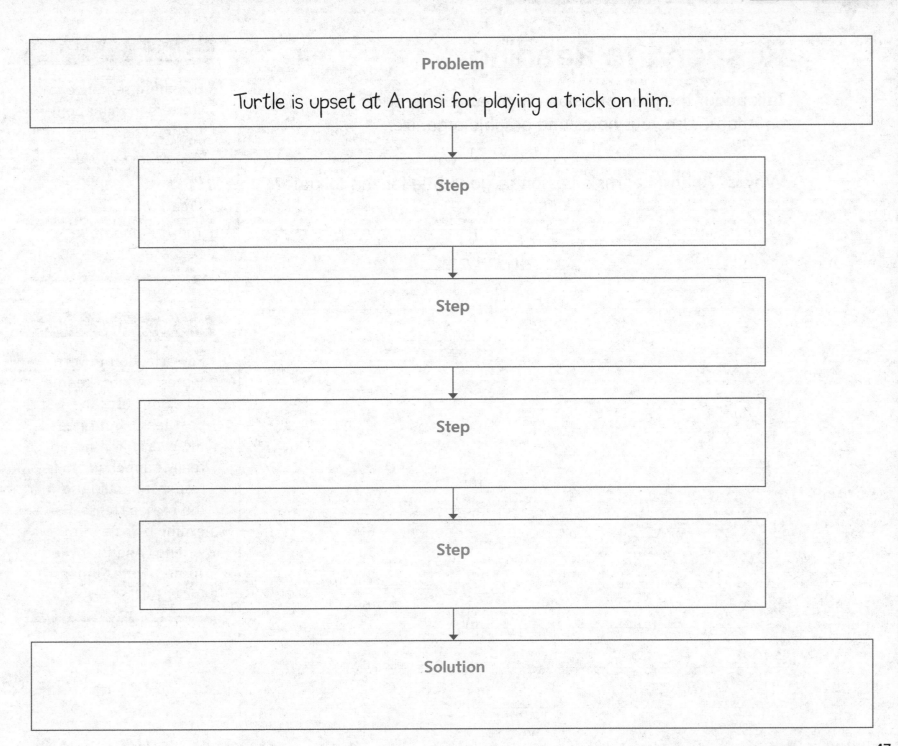

Problem

Turtle is upset at Anansi for playing a trick on him.

↓

Step

↓

Step

↓

Step

↓

Step

↓

Solution

Respond to Reading

Talk about the prompt below. Think about the trick Turtle plays on Anansi. Use your notes and graphic organizer.

Why is "Anansi Learns a Lesson" a good title for this folktale?

_____

_____

_____

_____

_____

_____

_____

_____

_____

_____

_____

_____

Quick Tip

Use these sentence starters to talk about the folktale.

Anansi tricks Turtle by . . .

I read that . . .

This is a good title because . . .

Grammar Connections

Pay attention to verb tenses. "Anansi Learns a Lesson" uses the past tense. But since the events in it never really happened, your response should use the present tense. For example, instead of writing "Anansi tricked Turtle," write, "Anansi tricks Turtle."

Key Words

Key words are precise words or phrases closely related to your topic. Using common words to research a topic online might give you information you can't use. But using precise key words helps you find relevant, or useful, information. Your teachers know a lot about your research topics and can help you think of key words.

Look at the diagram below. List key words that would help you find more information about frogs.

_____

What do the arrows help you understand?

_____

Draw a Life Cycle Choose an animal. Follow these steps to draw its life cycle.

1. Work with a science teacher or other adult to make a list of key words that will help you find images of and information about its life cycle.

2. Practice drawing each stage and write interesting facts about it in your own words.

3. Use the diagram on the right as a model to draw your animal's life cycle. Start by drawing the adult stage on the top left corner.

> **Quick Tip**
>
> Plants and animals go through changes throughout their lives. A life cycle diagram shows these changes, or stages, in sequence, or time order.

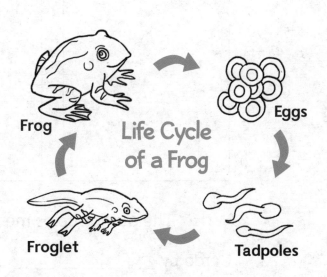

Frog · Eggs · Tadpoles · Froglet — Life Cycle of a Frog

SHUTTERSTOCK

Martina the Beautiful Cockroach

? How does the author help you visualize how Martina feels about Don Cerdo, the pig?

Literature Anthology: pages 212–231

Talk About It Reread page 223. Talk with a partner about how Don Cerdo smells to Martina and what she does.

Cite Text Evidence What clues help you understand how quickly Martina wants to get rid of Don Cerdo? Write text evidence and explain why it's important.

Evaluate Information

Notice the author's use of punctuation. How do exclamation points help you visualize how Don Cerdo smells?

Don Cerdo	What Martina Does	I Visualize

Write The author helps me visualize how Martina feels about Don

Cerdo by _____

_____

? How do you know what kind of character Don Lagarto is?

Talk About It Reread page 225. Talk with a partner about how the author describes Don Lagarto, the lizard.

Cite Text Evidence What clues help you get to know what the lizard is like? Write text evidence in the chart.

Clues	What It Means

Write I know what kind of character Don Lagarto is because the author _____

_____

_____

_____

Quick Tip

I can use these sentence starters when we talk about the lizard.

The author describes the lizard . . .

This makes me think he is . . .

Synthesize Information

Make connections between what happens earlier in the story and Martina's meeting with Don Lagarto. Talk about what kind of mood you think Martina is in when Don Lagarto shows up.

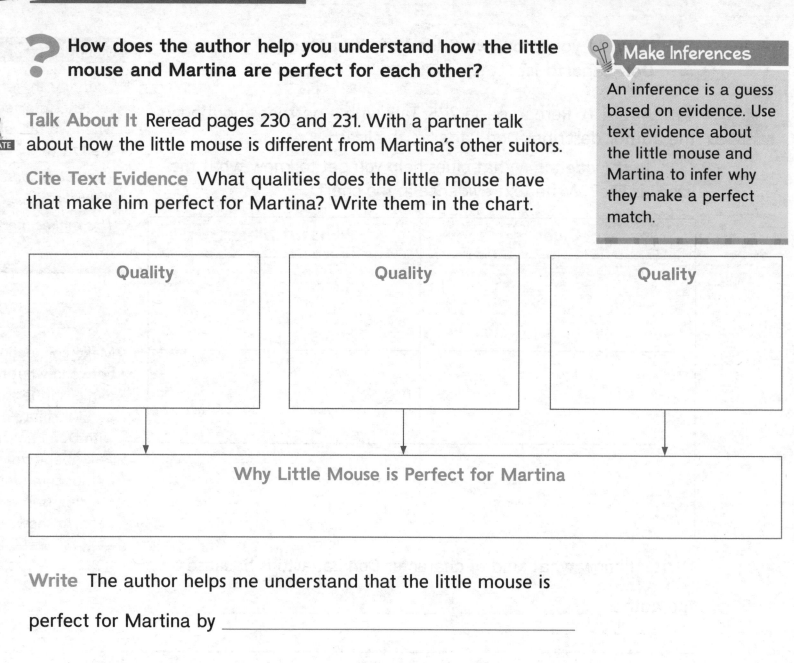

? **How does the author help you understand how the little mouse and Martina are perfect for each other?**

Make Inferences

An inference is a guess based on evidence. Use text evidence about the little mouse and Martina to infer why they make a perfect match.

Talk About It Reread pages 230 and 231. With a partner talk about how the little mouse is different from Martina's other suitors.

COLLABORATE

Cite Text Evidence What qualities does the little mouse have that make him perfect for Martina? Write them in the chart.

Quality	Quality	Quality

Why Little Mouse is Perfect for Martina

Write The author helps me understand that the little mouse is

perfect for Martina by _____

_____

_____

Respond to Reading

COLLABORATE

Answer the prompt below. Think about how the author's use of colorful details helps you understand what each character is like. Use your notes and graphic organizer.

How does Carmen Agra Deedy help you predict how the coffee test will turn out for each character?

_____

_____

_____

_____

_____

_____

_____

_____

_____

_____

Quick Tip

Use these sentence starters to talk about how the author reveals each character's traits.

Carmen Agra Deedy describes each animal by . . .

Then she . . .

This helps me understand why Martina . . .

Self-Selected Reading

Choose a text. In your writer's notebook, write the title, author, and genre of the book. As you read, make a connection to ideas in other texts you have read or to a personal experience. Write your ideas in your notebook.

Get a Backbone!

1   Most animals in the world fit in one of two groups. Some have backbones. The others do not. People, lizards, owls, frogs, and sharks all have backbones. Touch the back of your neck. That's where your backbone starts. It's a string of bones that goes all the way down your back to your tailbone.

2   What would you be like without a backbone? You couldn't walk or sit up. You'd have to slither around like a worm or swim like an octopus. Those animals have no backbones.

3   Animals with backbones are called vertebrates. All vertebrates have backbones. However, not all vertebrates are alike. They have different features. Some are tiny. Others are huge. Some swim, while others fly.

4   Vertebrates can be birds, amphibians, fish, reptiles, or mammals. Animals in each group share a unique quality that makes them special.

*Literature Anthology:
pages 234–237*

Reread and use the prompts to take notes in the text.

In paragraph 1, **draw a box around** how the author helps you understand what a backbone is. Look at the photograph. How does it help you understand more about the backbone?

_____

_____

_____

Reread paragraph 2. **Circle** words that help you visualize how animals without backbones move.

COLLABORATE

Reread paragraphs 3 and 4. With a partner, **underline** words and phrases the author uses to help you visualize different kinds of vertebrates.

Birds

5   Most birds can fly, but bees and bats can, too! Some birds, like ostriches and penguins, can't fly at all. Ostriches run. Penguins walk and swim. So what makes birds special?

6   Feathers, of course! Feathers keep birds warm. They can help birds to fly and steer through the air. The color of a bird's feathers can help it hide from predators or attract other birds.

Reptiles

7   Lizards and snakes are reptiles. All reptiles have scales covering their bodies

8   Because reptiles are cold-blooded, <u>they must live in warm places.</u> Some snakes, turtles, and crocodiles live mostly in warm water. <u>Some reptiles live in dry deserts.</u> Most reptiles have low bodies, four short legs, and a tail. Only snakes have no legs at all.

Reread paragraphs 5 and 6. **Write a number before** each sentence that says how birds can be different from each other. Then **circle** the sentence that states what all birds have in common.

COLLABORATE

Reread paragraph 8. Talk with a partner about what the word *cold-blooded* means. **Underline** how the author helps you understand what that means.

Then **draw a box around** two places where reptiles live. Write them here:

1 _____

2 _____

Steve Williams Photo/Stone/Getty Images

? How does the author organize information to help you understand vertebrates?

Talk About It Reread the excerpt on page 54. Talk with a partner about what the author does to make information about vertebrates easier to understand.

Cite Text Evidence How does the author organize information? Write evidence in the chart.

Quick Tip

As you reread each paragraph, look for sentences that help you understand or visualize its main idea.

Text Evidence	How It helps

Write The author helps me understand vertebrates by

_____

_____

Text Structure

Writers organize information to help readers understand their topic. They use text structure, like organization, to help readers figure out their purpose for writing.

🔍 FIND TEXT EVIDENCE

On page 55 of "Get a Backbone!" the author uses headings to organize information. By using headings, such as Birds, *the author lets you know that the section will be about birds.*

Birds

   Most birds can fly, but bees and bats can, too! Some birds, like ostriches and penguins, can't fly at all. Ostriches run. Penguins walk and swim. So what makes birds special?

COLLABORATE

Your Turn Reread the last two paragraphs on page 55.

- How does the author help you understand what reptiles are like?

  _____

  _____

- Why is "Reptiles" a good heading for this section? _____

  _____

Text Connections

? **How is the way George Stubbs painted a zebra like the way the authors of *Martina the Beautiful Cockroach* and "Get a Backbone!" describe different animals?**

Talk About It Look at the painting and read the caption. Talk with a partner about what makes this animal unique.

Cite Text Evidence Underline text evidence in the caption that tells how the zebra is unique. Circle two clues in the painting that show you. Think about how the authors of *Martina the Beautiful Cockroach* and "Get a Backbone!" used words and phrases to do the same.

Write Both the artist and the authors

describe animals by _____

_____

_____

_____

_____

_____

English artist George Stubbs painted "Zebra" in 1763. It's a painting of the first zebra to be seen in England. Stubbs made sure his painting looked exactly like the live animal by painting the zebra's ears facing backward and copying the stripes perfectly.

SCIENCE

Present Your Work

COLLABORATE

Decide how to present what you learned about an animal's life cycle to the class. You might create a poster or a digital slideshow. An adult can help you plan and put together a multimodal presentation, or a presentation that combines different media. Use the checklist to improve your presentation.

Tech Tip

A multimodal slide presentation allows you to present information in different ways. You can add images, audio clips, charts, and text to your slide show.

Before I present, I will practice my presentation by

_____

I think my presentation was _____

I know because _____

_____

_____

✓ Presenting Checklist

☐ I will make sure all the words in my poster or slideshow are spelled correctly.

☐ I will speak loudly so my audience can hear me.

☐ I will point to the information in the diagram.

☐ I will discuss each stage of my animal's life cycle in an understandable way.

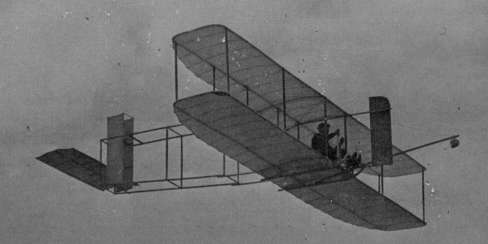

The Wright brothers tested their glider many times. Their experiments were important.

The Wright brothers tested one of their gliders in 1911 at Kitty Hawk, North Carolina. Their experiments helped make air travel today possible. History is made up of many unique events. Looking back at these events helps us appreciate what people went through to invent new things.

Look at the photograph. Talk about what makes this event unique. Write your ideas in the web.

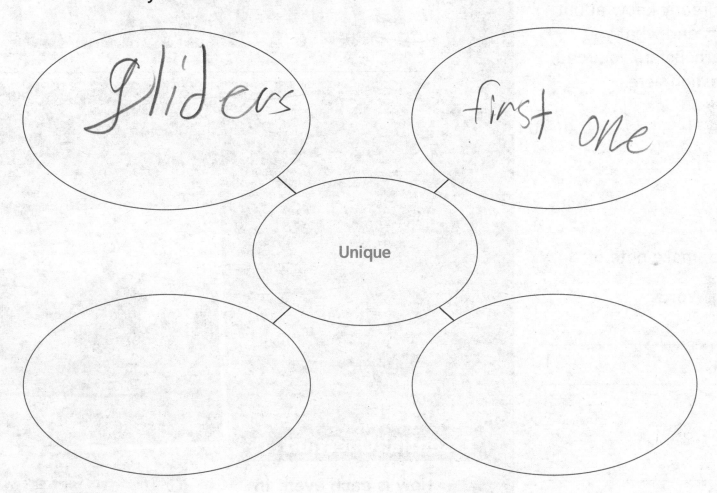

gliders

first one

Unique

Go online to **my.mheducation.com** and read "The Caddo" Blast. Think about how the Caddo people were unique. Then blast back your response.

TAKE NOTES

It is helpful to ask questions before you read. Asking questions helps you figure out what you already know about the first cars and what you want to learn. Before you read, write a question here.

What is it called?

As you read, make note of:

Interesting Words: _____

Key Details: _____

TIME FOR KIDS

Moving America
FORWARD

Essential Question

How is each event in history unique?

Read to see how the Model T changed the way people move.

Model T cars were strong and reliable. Many people in America drove them.

Henry Ford introduced the Ford Model T car in 1908. The original **vehicles** came in blue, gray, green, and red. They cost $850 to buy. Everyone wanted a Model T, and thanks to the moving assembly line, almost everyone could have one. By 1918, half of all cars in the United States were Model Ts.

Everybody Wants One

The Model T was not the first car ever made, but it was the one most people could afford to buy at the time. One of the **resources** Ford used to build the Model T was steel. The car, which was nicknamed "Tin Lizzie," was built to hold up on rough roads. It was dependable and easy to drive. They were also simple to maintain, or fix. As the nation's **population** grew, more and more people were buying cars. They wanted to own a Model T.

Before the Model T, cars were expensive. Not everyone had enough money to own one. Ford knew that he needed to bring the price down. First he found a way to make more cars to meet the demand. Then he made them faster. Finally, he was able to make them affordable, or lower the cost so more people could buy one.

The first Model T hit the roads on October 1, 1908. It could travel at a speed of 45 miles per hour.

FIND TEXT EVIDENCE

Read

Paragraph 1

Summarize

Underline details about the Ford Model T car. Summarize the text in your own words.

The Model T was made in 1908. They cost $850 dollars.

Paragraph 2

Suffixes

Draw a box around the word *dependable*. Write what *dependable* means.

able

Paragraph 3

Sequence

Circle steps Ford took to lower the price of the Model T car.

Reread

Author's Craft

Reread the second paragraph. How does the author help you understand what *maintain* means?

SHARED READ

FIND TEXT EVIDENCE

Read

Paragraph 1

Summarize

Underline how Ford improved the assembly line. Then summarize in your own words.

ford made cars go faster an 8 workers build cars in one hour ans 33 minutes.

Paragraph 2

Sequence

Draw a box around what happened after the engines and gas tanks were added.

Timelines

What happened in 1915?

cars stoped at the first stop sign.

Circle the year cars first used turn signals.

Reread

Author's Craft

How does the author help you understand how an assembly line works?

TIME FOR KIDS

These workers on an assembly line are putting together Model T cars in Detroit, Michigan, in 1927.

Assembly Required

Henry Ford did not invent the assembly line. But in 1913, he improved on it. Ford rolled out a moving assembly line that made building cars much faster. One Model T used to take more than 12 hours to build. Using a moving assembly line, workers could build a car in one hour and 33 minutes.

To build a Model T, workers and machines worked together. There were 84 steps. First, some workers stood at assembly stations putting small car parts together. Then, a moving conveyer belt carried the car parts along as more workers put them together. After that, the body of the car was pulled along as more workers put their parts onto it. Then the engines and gas tanks were added. Finally, the car bodies were assembled, and the car was finished.

The moving assembly line changed **transportation** in the United States. Workers could build many cars at once. Business **boomed**.

Many inventions have made it safer for people to drive cars.

Timeline: Drive Safely

1880	1890	1900	1910

1885
The first seatbelts were used.

1903
Mary Anderson invented the windshield wiper.

---

64   Unit 3 · Expository Text

A World on Wheels

The price of the Model T dropped to less than $300 in 1925. More and more people bought them. As a result, more roads and highways were paved. Then gas stations and hotels sprung up. Next, many people moved out of cities. The people who lived in the 1920s started to **appreciate** being able to drive to work or go on a journey. Driving around was an **agreeable** way for them to spend time. Their **descendants** today may find life before cars hard to imagine.

Mary Anderson and the Windshield Wiper

Mary Anderson invented the windshield wiper while riding a streetcar in 1902 during a snowstorm in New York City.

After watching her streetcar driver jump in and out of the streetcar to clear off his icy windshield, Mary had an idea. First she sketched her idea. Next she worked out a plan. Then, Mary built a model out of rubber, wood, and metal. Finally, in 1903 she tested it. It worked!

By 1913, more people bought cars. Thanks to Mary Anderson, they had windshield wipers.

Summarize

Use your notes and think about the most important ideas in "Moving America Forward." Summarize them.

1920   1930   1940

1915
Cars stopped at the first stop sign.

STOP

1938
Cars first used turn signals.

(bl)Richard Allen/Flair Talent/Image Source;(t)Popperfoto/Getty Images;(bc) Image Source/Getty Images;(br) Bettmann/Getty Images

FIND TEXT EVIDENCE

Read

Paragraph 1
Sequence
What happened after gas stations and hotels sprung up?

Next many people moved out of cities.

Circle the signal word.

Sidebars
How did Mary get the idea to invent the windshield wiper?

During a snowstorm in New York city.

Underline text evidence.

Reread

Author's Craft

Why is "A World on Wheels" a good heading for this section?

Vocabulary

Use the sentences to talk with a partner about each word. Then answer the questions.

agreeable

Eric loves warm weather that is pleasant and **agreeable**.

What kind of weather do you find agreeable?

_____

_____

appreciate

Jan and Kayla **appreciate** everything their grandmother does for them.

How do you show people that you appreciate them?

_____

_____

> **Build Your Word List** Pick one of the interesting words you listed on page 62. Use a print or online dictionary to find the word's meaning. Then make a list of words that mean almost the same.

boomed

Juan's lemonade business **boomed** in the summer, and he sold more lemonade than ever before.

Boomed has multiple meanings. Can you name another word with multiple meanings?

_____

_____

descendants

Ann and her family are **descendants** of the people in the photographs.

What are descendants?

_____

_____

resources

Plants need **resources**, such as sunlight and fresh air, to grow.

What resources do people need?

_____

_____

population

There is a large **population** of flamingos living in the pond.

Name another animal population that might live in a pond.

_____

_____

transportation

Trains are a favorite form of **transportation** for many people.

Write a sentence about your favorite form of transportation.

_____

_____

vehicles

Vehicles are parked in a parking lot.

What type of vehicle do you travel to school in?

_____

_____

Suffixes

A suffix is a word part added to the end of a word. It changes the word's meaning. The suffix *-able* means "is or can be."

🔍 FIND TEXT EVIDENCE

I see the word agreeable *on page 65.* Agreeable *has the root word* agree. *I know that* agree *means "to be pleasing." The suffix* -able *means "is able or can be." I think the word* agreeable *means "can be pleasing."*

Driving around was an agreeable way for them to spend time.

Your Turn Use the suffix to figure out the meaning of the word.

affordable, page 63 _____

_____

_____

Summarize

When you summarize, you tell the most important ideas and details in a text. Use details to help you summarize "Moving America Forward."

🔍 FIND TEXT EVIDENCE

Why did many people want to buy the Model T car? Reread "Everybody Wants One" on page 63. Evaluate and decide which details are most important. Then use the key ideas to summarize the text in your own words.

Page 63

Everybody Wants One

The Model T was not the first car ever made, but it was the one most people could afford to buy at the time. One of the **resources** Ford used to build the Model T was steel. The car, which was nicknamed "Tin Lizzie," was built to hold up on rough roads. It was dependable and easy to drive. They were also simple to maintain, or fix. As the nation's **population** grew, more and more people were buying cars. They wanted to own a Model T.

I read that the Model T was the car _most people could afford to buy_. The Model T _was dependable and easy to drive. It was also simple to maintain, or fix._ These key details are important. They help me summarize. Many people wanted to buy the Model T because it didn't cost too much and it was easy to drive and take care of.

Your Turn Reread "Assembly Required" on page 64. Use the key details to summarize the text. Then write your summary here.

_____

_____

Timelines and Captions

"Moving America Forward" is an **expository text**. An expository text

- may explain a social studies or science topic
- has headings and sidebars
- may include photographs, captions, sidebars, and timelines.

FIND TEXT EVIDENCE

I can tell that "Moving America Forward" is an expository text. It gives information about Henry Ford and the Model T car. It also has photographs, captions, a sidebar, and a timeline.

Readers to Writers

Writers use captions to provide more information that will help readers understand more about the topic. When you write captions, include information that is not in the text.

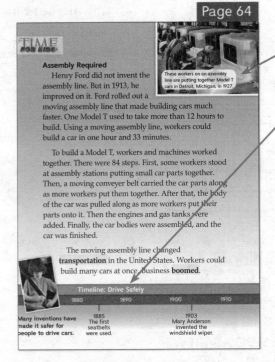

Page 64

TIME FOR KIDS

Assembly Required

Henry Ford did not invent the assembly line. But in 1913, he improved on it. Ford rolled out a moving assembly line that made building cars much faster. One Model T used to take more than 12 hours to build. Using a moving assembly line, workers could build a car in one hour and 33 minutes.

To build a Model T, workers and machines worked together. There were 84 steps. First, some workers stood at assembly stations putting small car parts together. Then, a moving conveyer belt carried the car parts along as more workers put them together. After that, the body of the car was pulled along as more workers put their parts onto it. Then the engines and gas tanks were added. Finally, the car bodies were assembled, and the car was finished.

The moving assembly line changed **transportation** in the United States. Workers could build many cars at once. Business **boomed**.

These workers on an assembly line are putting together Model T cars in Detroit, Michigan, in 1927.

Timeline: Drive Safely

1880　　1890　　1900　　1910

Many inventions have made it safer for people to drive cars.

1885 The first seatbelts were used.

1903 Mary Anderson invented the windshield wiper.

Captions

Photographs and captions give additional facts and details.

Timeline

A timeline shows the time order in which important dates and events happened.

COLLABORATE

Your Turn Look at the timeline on page 64. In what year were seatbelts first used? Write your answer here.

_____

Sequence

Sequence is the order in which important events take place. Look for words and phrases that show time order, such as *first, next, then, later that day, after that,* and *finally*. These signal words show the sequence of events.

🔍 FIND TEXT EVIDENCE

In "Moving America Forward," the author describes how the Model T was assembled on an assembly line in time order. The signal word first *shows what happened first. The workers put small car parts together. I can use other signal words to understand the order of the steps.*

Quick Tip

Authors can also use dates to show sequence, or time order. In the first paragraph on page 63, the year 1908 tells when Henry Ford first introduced the Model T car. Later in the paragraph, the year 1918 shows that ten years later, half of all the cars in the U.S. were Model T cars.

Event
First, workers put together small car parts.

↓

Event
Then a conveyor belt carried the parts to other workers.

↓

Event
After that, the body of the car was pulled along as more workers put their parts onto it.

Your Turn Reread the sidebar on page 65. List the steps Mary Anderson took to invent the windshield wiper. Write the steps in order in your graphic organizer. Use signal words.

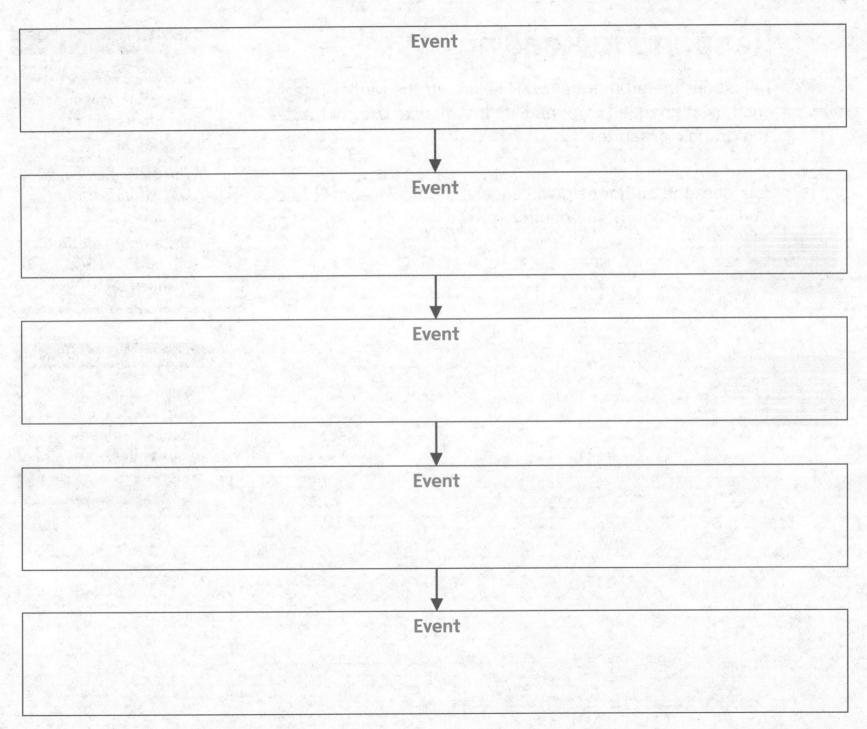

Event

Event

Event

Event

Event

Respond to Reading

COLLABORATE

Talk about the prompt below. Think about the Model T car and how it changed work and life in America. Use your notes and graphic organizer.

How does the author help you understand how Henry Ford's Model T car moved America forward?

_____

_____

_____

_____

_____

_____

_____

_____

_____

Quick Tip

Use these sentence starters to talk about the Model T car.

I read that . . .

The moving assembly line was important because . . .

The author helps me see how America changed by . . .

Grammar Connections

As you write your response, try to combine some of your sentences using interesting verbs.

Giving and Following Instructions

Instructions describe how to do or make something. When writing instructions, it is important to:

• provide steps that are easy to follow
• use time-order words to make the order of the steps clear

Read and follow these instructions with a partner.

Will It Fly?
1. First, fold two paper airplanes. Make the wing sizes different.
2. Then, gently throw one plane.
3. Next, measure and record how far the plane flew.
4. Repeat the experiment with the other plane.

COLLABORATE

Write Instructions Think of something simple you know how to do. Write three or four steps of instructions telling how to do it. Use time-order words. Then read your instructions to a partner. Have them restate and follow them. Then switch.

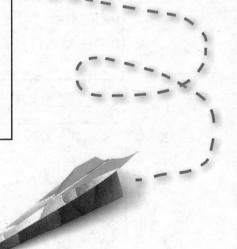

Ken Karp/McGraw-Hill Education

Birth of an Anthem

 How does the way the author organizes the text help me understand how America's national anthem was created?

Literature Anthology: pages 238–241

 Talk About It Reread pages 240 and 241. Talk with a partner about what inspired Francis Scott Key to write "The Star-Spangled Banner."

Cite Text Evidence What clues does the author use to help you understand the cause and effect structure? Write text evidence in the chart.

Cause	→	Effect

Write The author organizes the text to help me understand _____

_____

_____

How does the sidebar help you understand where America's patriotic anthems come from?

Talk About It Reread the sidebar on page 240. Talk with a partner about how the sidebar helps you understand what unofficial anthems are.

Cite Text Evidence How is the information in the sidebar different from what you read in the selection? Find examples in the text.

Birth of an Anthem	Sidebar

Write The author uses the sidebar to help me understand that

_____

_____

_____

Respond to Reading

Answer the prompt below. Think about how the author organizes information. Use your notes and graphic organizer.

How does the author help you understand how Francis Scott Key wrote "The Star-Spangled Banner"?

_____

_____

_____

_____

_____

_____

_____

_____

_____

_____

Quick Tip

Use these sentence starters to talk about Francis Scott Key.

The author organizes information to . . .

The author also uses a sidebar to . . .

This helps me see that . . .

Self-Selected Reading

Choose a text. In your writer's notebook, write the title, author, and genre of the book. As you read, make a connection to ideas in other texts you read, or to a personal experience. Write your ideas in your notebook.

Discovering Life Long Ago

Literature Anthology:
pages 242–243

1   In the past, people wrote in diaries and journals. They wrote letters to friends and families. They also wrote autobiographies to tell their life stories. Diaries, journals, and autobiographies tell us what people thought and felt. They also give details about daily life in the past. They describe the food people ate. They tell what kind of transportation they used.

2   Posters, newspapers, and old photographs also give details about events in the past. So do speeches and songs. Photographs show people's clothes and how they had fun.

3   Both words and pictures from the past help us see how people lived long ago. They tell a history of people, places, and things. They take us back in time.

Reread and use the prompts to take notes in the text.

Reread paragraphs 1 and 2. **Underline** the ways people used to tell about the way life was long ago. In the margin, **number** the different things we can learn. List three of them here:

1 _____

2 _____

3 _____

COLLABORATE

Turn and talk with a partner about how the author organized the information in this selection. **Circle** the paragraph that summarizes all the information.

? **How does the author help you understand how people learn about events in the past?**

Talk About It Reread paragraphs 1 and 2 on page 77. Talk with a partner about the ways people learn more about the past.

Cite Text Evidence How does the author arrange the information to help you understand how we learn about life long ago? Write text evidence here.

Quick Tip

When I reread, I can use the way the author shares information to help me understand the topic better.

Paragraph 1	Paragraph 2	This Helps Because...

Write The author helps me understand how people learn about

the past by _____

_____

_____

_____

_____

_____

Point of View

Writers use third-person point of view when telling about something that happened. People who describe something that happened to them tell their story in first-person point of view.

 FIND TEXT EVIDENCE

On page 77 of "Discovering Life Long Ago," the author uses the words *they* and *their* to tell the story of what life was like long ago. The author is using third-person point of view.

> In the past, people wrote in diaries and journals. They wrote letters to friends and families. They also wrote autobiographies to tell their life stories.

COLLABORATE

Your Turn Reread Sallie Hester's diary entry on page 243 of "Discovering Life Long Ago" in the **Literature Anthology**.

• How do you know that Sallie's diary is written in first-person point of view? _____

_____

• How does the author help you understand the way people lived long ago? _____

_____

A diary is an example of a primary source. Information from primary sources helps readers understand what it was like to actually experience events from the past.

Text Connections

? **How do the song lyrics help you visualize an event in history in the same way the words and phrases in "Birth of an Anthem" and "Discovering Life Long Ago" do?**

Talk About It Read the song lyrics. Talk with a partner about what Betsy and her brother did.

Cite Text Evidence

Circle words and phrases in the song lyrics that tell who went on the journey and what creatures they brought with them. **Underline** clues that show what they did.

Write The song lyrics help me visualize the

journey by _____

_____

_____

_____

_____

_____

from Sweet Betsy from Pike

Oh, do you remember sweet
  Betsy from Pike,
Who crossed the wide prairies
  with her brother Ike?
With two yoke of oxen, a
  big yaller dog,
A tall Shanghai rooster and
  one spotted hog. . . .

They camped on the prairie for
  weeks upon weeks.
They swam the wide rivers and
  crossed the tall peaks.
And soon they were rollin' in
  nuggets of gold.
You may not believe it but
  that's what we're told.

American Folk Song
Adapted by Merrill Staton

Accuracy and Phrasing

Think about the meaning of the text. Focus on your *accuracy* by reading each word correctly. Sound out longer words and read them slowly. *Phrasing* means to read groups of related words together. Use punctuation marks, such as commas, to identify phrases. This will help you know where to pause while reading.

Page 63

Henry Ford introduced the Ford Model T car in 1908. The vehicles came in blue, gray, green, and red.

The commas in this text signal places to briefly pause while reading.

Your Turn Turn back to page 63. Take turns reading the first paragraph aloud with a partner. Read each word correctly. Use punctuation to help you read related groups of words together and pause after each phrase.

Afterward, think about how you did. Complete these sentences.

I remembered to _____

_____

Next time I will _____

_____

_____

*Literature Anthology:
pages 238–241*

Expert Model

Features of a Feature Article

A **feature article** is a kind of expository text. A feature article

- tells about a current event or topic of interest

- uses paragraphs to give facts, definitions, and details that explain the topic

- has an opening that grabs the readers' attention and a concluding statement that gives readers something to think about

Analyze an Expert Model Feature articles give information about an interesting topic. Reread the first paragraph of "Birth of an Anthem" on page 239 in the **Literature Anthology**. Use text evidence to answer the questions.

What does the author do that grabs your attention and makes you want to read more? _____

_____

Why is "It Began in Baltimore" a good heading for this section?

_____

_____

Word Wise

Writers use paragraphs to group ideas that tell important information about a topic. A well-written paragraph will include a great topic sentence, supporting details, and transition words. For example, the first sentence of "Birth of an Anthem" is an interesting fact. Then the author uses the transition word, *but*, to connect it with a supporting detail.

Plan: Choose Your Topic

Brainstorm With a partner, brainstorm a list of people, events, or symbols that have been important to life in the United States. Think about the sequence of events that made them important to us today. Use the sentence starters below to talk about your ideas.

A person or event that has formed the U.S. is . . .

This became an important part of our history when . . .

Writing Prompt Choose a person, event, or symbol that you think was important in the history of the United States. Remember to think about the specific details and events that made this person, event, or symbol important.

I will write about _____.

Purpose and Audience An author's purpose is the main reason for writing. Your audience is the people who will be reading your feature article.

The reason I am writing about this topic is _____

_____

_____

Plan Think about what you want your readers to know about your topic. Draw a Sequence chart in your writer's notebook. Write one important event in the first box.

Quick Tip

Remember that you will be describing the events that helped this historical person, event, or symbol become important to the United States. A well-organized article will describe these events in sequential order. Remember to use time-order words to describe the order of events in your article.

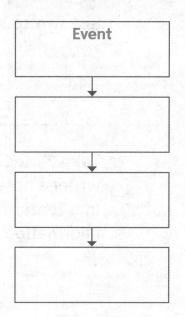

Event

Plan: Research

Identify Relevant Information When writing a feature article, writers need to research their topic before they can begin. They use reliable sources such as encyclopedias, websites, interviews, books, and magazines to find this information. Then they decide if the information they found is relevant, or related to what they are writing about.

To check that your sources are reliable and relevant, answer these questions:

- Is the information accurate and current?
- Does the information provide what I need to know about my topic?
- Is the material too difficult? Do I need to find another source?

List two sources that you will use.

1. _____

2. _____

Take Notes Once you pick your sources, take notes. In your writer's notebook, fill in the Sequence chart to plan your writing. In a feature article, ideas are presented in order. Organizing your information will help your readers make sense of the text.

Quick Tip

Work with a teacher, or another adult, to create a plan for your research. You can check in with an adult as you conduct your research to be sure that your sources are reliable and relevant.

Draft

COLLABORATE

Clear Central Idea Writers use a clear central idea to tell about a topic. This idea is usually introduced in the first sentence. The author then includes supporting facts and details to develop the idea. Reread the sidebar on page 240 in the **Literature Anthology**. Use text evidence to answer the questions below.

What is the central idea of the first paragraph?

_____

_____

How does the author support this idea?

_____

_____

How does the author help you understand the importance of a patriotic song?

_____

_____

_____

Write a Draft Use your Sequence chart to help you write your draft in your writer's notebook. Remember to include a clear central idea and supporting facts and details.

Grammar Connections

Writers combine sentences that have the same subject but different verbs. By combining these two sentences into one, the writer makes the text easier to read and understand. Look at this example from "Birth of an Anthem":

"He *boarded* the British ship and *persuaded* the British to free the doctor."

Revise

Quick Tip

Writers may add text features such as photographs, captions, timelines, or even diary entries to make a feature article more interesting to read and easier to understand.

Strong Conclusion Writers end a feature article with a strong conclusion. This conclusion summarizes the main idea and details. The writer may also leave the reader with something to think about by using a statement, a question, or even text features.

Reread page 242 in the **Literature Anthology.** Talk with a partner about how the author ended this part of the article. How do the conclusion and poster give the reader something to think about? Write about it here.

_____

_____

_____

Revise It's time to revise your writing. Read your draft and look for places where you might:

- make the central idea of a paragraph clearer

- make your conclusion stronger

Circle two sentences from your draft that you can change. Revise and write them here.

1 _____

2 _____

Peer Conferences

Review a Draft Listen carefully as a partner reads his or her draft aloud. Tell what you like about the draft. Use these sentence starters to help you discuss your partner's draft.

I like this part because it helped me to understand . . .

Add another fact or detail here to explain . . .

I didn't understand the sequence of events because . . .

I have a question about . . .

Partner Feedback After you take turns giving each other feedback, write one of the suggestions from your partner that you will use in your revision.

_____

_____

_____

_____

Revision After you finish your peer conference, use the Revising Checklist to help you figure out what you can change to make your feature article better. Remember to use the rubric on page 89 to help you with your revision.

Revising Checklist

☐ Does each paragraph have a clear central idea?

☐ Does my article include a logical sequence of events?

☐ Did I include facts, definitions, and details to explain the topic of my article?

☐ Is my essay well organized into paragraphs with a strong opening and conclusion?

Tech Tip

If you wrote your draft on a computer, it is easy to move sentences around or add facts and details to your draft without starting over.

Edit and Proofread

After you revise your feature article, proofread it to find any mistakes in grammar, spelling, and punctuation. Read your draft at least three times. This will help you catch any mistakes. Use the checklist below to edit your sentences.

✔ Editing Checklist

☐ Do all sentences begin with a capital letter and end with a punctuation mark?

☐ Are there sentences where the same subject is combined with different verbs?

☐ Are there capital letters at the beginning of proper nouns?

☐ Are all words spelled correctly?

Grammar Connections

When you proofread your draft for mistakes, remember to use a capital letter at the beginning of proper nouns. Historical figures, events, and symbols such as *George Washington,* the *War of 1812,* and *"The Star-Spangled Banner"* are all proper nouns.

List two mistakes that you found as you proofread your feature article.

1 _____

_____

_____

2 _____

_____

_____

Publish, Present, and Evaluate

Publishing When you publish your writing, you create a neat final copy that is free of mistakes. If you are not using a computer, use your best handwriting. Write legibly in print or cursive.

Presentation When you are ready to present, practice your presentation. Use the Presenting Checklist.

Evaluate After you publish, use the rubric to evaluate it.

What did you do successfully? _____

_____

What needs more work? _____

_____

4	3	2	1
• includes clear introduction, many details, and a strong conclusion • presents events in correct order • all proper nouns are capitalized and spelled correctly	• includes introduction, some details, and a conclusion • presents events in correct order • most proper nouns are capitalized and spelled correctly	• introduction or conclusion may be missing, includes only a few details • some events are out of order • several capitalization or spelling errors	• no introduction; supporting details and conclusion may be missing • most events are out of order • numerous capitalization and spelling errors

Spiral Review

You have learned new skills and strategies in Unit 3 that will help you read more critically. Now it is time to practice what you have learned.

- Suffixes
- Summarize
- Main Idea and Key Details
- Context Clues
- Visualize
- Problem and Solution
- Sequence
- Metaphors

Connect to Content

- Create a Timeline
- Select a Genre
- Read Digitally

Read the selection and choose the best answer to each question.

Fascinating Facts About Our Amazing Sun

[1] If you are like a lot of people, you take the Sun for granted. You might even complain that it is too hot or too bright. But without the Sun, there would be no life on Earth. It gives us light. It keeps us warm. It grows our food. If there were no Sun, Earth would be nothing more than a big ball of ice.

[2] Here are some other fascinating facts about the Sun.

[3] The Sun is the center of our solar system. All eight planets, their moons, and other objects in the solar system orbit, or circle around, the Sun.

[4] The Sun is a star, or a body of hot gases that makes and gives off heat and light energy. This energy provides the light and heat that all life needs to survive on Earth.

[5] The Sun has gravity, or an invisible force that pulls objects toward it. The Sun's gravity holds the solar system together. It keeps everything, from the largest planets to the tiniest pieces of dust, in the Sun's orbit.

6   The Sun is the largest object in our solar system. It is about one million times bigger than Earth. However, it is not the largest star in the galaxy. It seems extremely big to us because, at 93 million miles away, it is closer to us than any other star.

7   The Sun also influences the daily rise and fall of ocean waters, weather, climate, and many other natural wonders.

8   Sunlight can be harmful to your eyes and skin. It is never a good idea to look directly at the Sun, or to be outside too long without protection, such as sunglasses. Applying sunscreen to your skin is also important. Too much sunlight on unprotected skin can lead to serious diseases, including skin cancer.

9   The Sun contributes to good health, too. It helps the body make vitamin D, which is vital to the body.

10   The next time you think the Sun is a bother, remember how important it is to all life on Earth!

Astronomers use special telescopes to see solar flares on the surface of the Sun.

1 Which sentence best states the main idea of paragraph 1?

  A A lot of people take the Sun for granted.

  B Without the Sun, there would be no life on Earth.

  C If there were no Sun, Earth would be a big ball of ice.

  D The Sun gives us light and heat.

2 In paragraph 6, the suffix -*ly* changes the meaning of the word *extreme* to:

  F less extreme

  G more extreme

  H able to be extreme

  J in an extreme way

3 Which sentence best summarizes the passage?

  A The Sun is a large star.

  B The Sun is the center of the solar system.

  C The Sun is fascinating.

  D The Sun is important to all life on Earth.

4 In paragraph 3, which context clue helps you understand the meaning of *orbit*?

  F invisible

  G force

  H circle around

  J dust

> **Quick Tip**
>
> Context clues are the words and sentences around an unknown word that help you figure out what the word means. Synonyms, or words that have the same meaning, are context clues.

Read the selection and choose the best answer to each question.

The Cheetah's Tears

1.   Long ago, a hunter needed to hunt to feed his hungry family. Soon he spied an antelope that had strayed from its herd. The hunter prepared to catch his prey. Then all at once, a cheetah sprinted out of the grass and pounced on the antelope. She then dragged it away to her den, where three hungry cubs waited for her return.

2.   The sight of the cubs gave the hunter an idea. He was impressed with the cheetah's speed and hunting ability. He thought, "I could train a cheetah cub to hunt for me. Then my family would never be hungry again."

3.   A few days later, the mother cheetah was off on another hunt. The hunter took the opportunity to raid her den. He was going to steal one cub, but had another thought. "I will take all three. Three could hunt for a lot more food for my family." With that, he collected the three cubs in his arms and ran back to his village.

4   When the mother cheetah returned to her den, her jaw dropped. Her fresh catch fell to the ground. After a quick look around, she knew her cubs were gone. Her heart was filled with sadness and she cried and cried. Rivers of tears streamed from her eyes for so long they left dark stains down her cheeks.

5   An old man heard the cheetah crying. "What is wrong?" he asked her.

6   "My cubs are missing," she sobbed.

7   The man quickly realized that he had seen the cubs in his village earlier that day. He promised he would bring her babies back.

8   The old man found the hunter who had stolen the cubs. He wanted to train them to hunt for him. The old man scolded him, "How dare you dishonor our tribe's tradition of using your own ability and skills to hunt!" He took the cubs from the hunter and quickly returned them to their mother.

9   The mother cheetah's heart filled with happiness. However, the hours of crying left her face permanently stained. And that is why cheetahs have dark stripes on their faces.

1 Which sentence best states the hunter's main problem?

A He needed to hunt for his hungry family.

B He wanted a cheetah to help him hunt.

C The cheetah caught his prey before he did.

D The old man made him return the cubs.

2 In paragraph 4, what happens first after the mother cheetah returns to her den?

F She looks around.

G Her jaw drops.

H She knows her cubs are gone.

J She starts to cry.

3 In paragraph 4, what type of figurative language does the author use to help readers visualize the cheetah's tears?

A simile

B metaphor

C onomatopoeia

D personification

Quick Tip

Authors use figurative language to help readers visualize, or picture, a story's characters, events, and settings.

4 Which word in paragraph 9 has a suffix that means "the state of being?"

F happiness

G filled

H crying

J permanently

COMPARING GENRES

- In the **Literature Anthology**, reread the folktale *Martina the Beautiful Cockroach* on pages 212–231, and the expository text, "Get a Backbone!" on pages 234–237.

- Use the Venn diagram below to show how the two genres are alike and different.

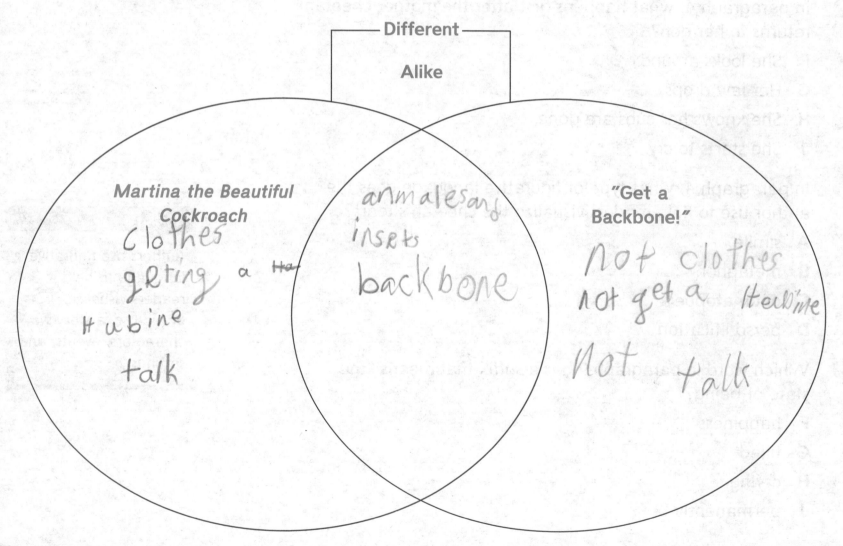

Different

Alike

Martina the Beautiful Cockroach

Clothes
geting a Ha
Hubine

talk

anmalesan
insets

backbone

"Get a Backbone!"

not clothes
not get a Hewine

Not talk

SYNONYMS

COLLABORATE

Synonyms are words that have similar meanings. Sometimes you can use them as context clues to figure out words you don't know.

- Read each sentence below.

- Circle the synonym that helps you understand the boldfaced word.

- Then, use a print or online thesaurus to find another synonym for each word and write it on the line.

Gigantic and **huge** are synonyms.

1. The actress's **ruby** dress matched the red curtains behind her.

Synonym: _____

2. Martin was **perplexed** by the problem. It puzzled me, too.

Synonym: _____

3. Sal was so **exhausted** that he was too tired to get out bed.

Synonym: _____

4. Layla told her father of her **conundrum,** but he could not help

her with the problem.

Synonym: _____

5. I felt **remorse** for breaking Art's bike, but I was not sure how to

tell him I was sorry.

Synonym: _____

CREATE A TIMELINE

A timeline shows the order in which key events happened during a certain time period. Timelines can be vertical or horizontal.

- Research a famous inventor or scientist who created a new technology or discovered a scientific breakthrough.
- Create a timeline of the important events in his or her life.

The inventor or scientist I chose to research is _____

An important event in this person's life was _____

because _____

SELECT A GENRE

When presenting information, it's important to choose a genre that fits your purpose.

- Research one planet in the solar system and its position in relation to the Sun. Then find two interesting facts about it.
- Decide how to present your research. Think about whether you want to inform people or entertain them. Then, choose a genre, such as expository essay or poem, that best fits your purpose.
- Plan your draft by freewriting or mapping your ideas in an idea web. Revise and edit your draft and present it to an audience.

Something I learned about my planet that I did not know before is

_____

_____

SAVING OUR OCEANS

Log on to **my.mheducation.com** and read the Time for Kids online article "Saving Our Oceans" including the information found in the interactive elements. Answer the questions below.

Saving Our Oceans

One woman is working to save our oceans the simple way, by protecting them.

Sylvia Earle is a marine scientist. She is worried about the oceans. For more than 50 years, she has observed them, dived into them, and written about them. But now Earle is using her knowledge to help save them.

Ahead of Her Time

Sylvia Earle was born in 1935 in New Jersey. When she was a young girl, she loved to hike in the woods with her family. She learned about the animals that lived there. She learned to respect them. Then, when she was 13 years old, her family moved to Florida. There she fell in love with the ocean and the animals that lived in and around it.

Living near the ocean made Earle very happy. When she turned 17 years old, she started scuba diving. Earle spent thousands of hours under the sea. She even

Time for Kids: "Saving Our Oceans"

- What text structure does the author use to organize the information in this article? Why do you think the author chose this text structure? _____

_____

_____

- How do the photographs in the article help you better understand the text?

_____

_____

- What is the author's purpose for including a link to the Mission Blue website?

_____

_____

sharppy/Shutterstock

TRACK YOUR PROGRESS

WHAT DID YOU LEARN?

Use the Rubric to evaluate yourself on the skills that you learned in this unit. Write your scores in the boxes below.

4	3	2	1
I can successfully identify all examples of this skill.	I can identify most examples of this skill.	I can identify a few examples of this skill.	I need to work on this skill more.

☐ Main Idea and Key Details   ☐ Problem and Solution   ☐ Sequence

☐ Suffixes   ☐ Synonyms

Something I need to work more on is _____ because

_____

_____

Text-to-Self Think back over the texts that you have read in this unit. Choose one text and write a short paragraph explaining a personal connection that you have made to the text. This will help you better understand the text.

I made a personal connection to _____ because _____

_____

SOCIAL STUDIES

Present Your Work

COLLABORATE

Discuss how you will present your instructions to the class. Use the Presenting Checklist as you practice your presentation. Discuss the sentence starters below and write your answers.

The step that is hardest in my instructions is _____

_____

_____

I would like to like to learn the instructions for _____

because _____

_____

Talk About It

We all have skills and talents. We might be artistic or good at sports. We can use our talents to help others. Our skills and talents make us feel good about ourselves.

Look at the photograph. Talk with a partner about how people use their talents to help others. Write your ideas in the web.

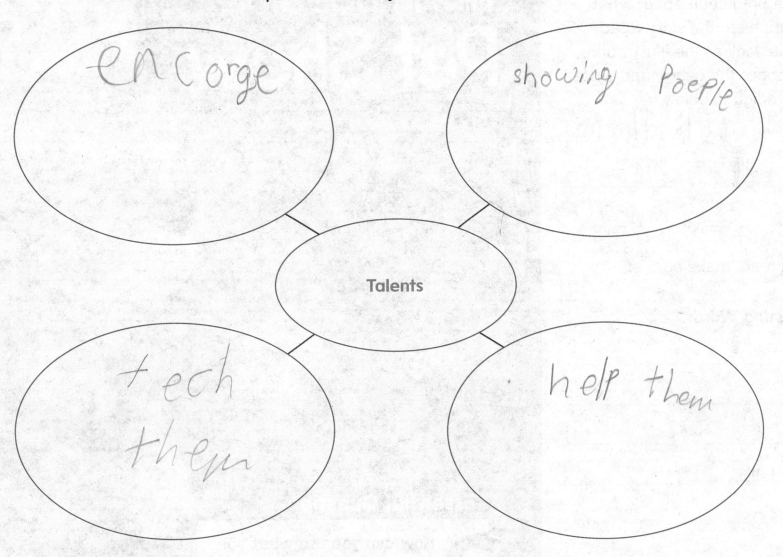

encorge

showing poeple

Talents

tech them

help them

Go online to **my.mheducation.com** and read the "Clara Barton" Blast. Think about how Clara Barton helped others. Then blast back your response.

TAKE NOTES

To help you focus as you read, make a prediction about what will happen in the story. Read the title, look at the illustrations, think about the genre, and write your prediction below.

The girl think a pet show imposs and things can go bad?

As you read, make note of:

Interesting Words: _____

_____

_____

_____

Key Details: _____

_____

_____

_____

The Impossible Pet Show

Essential Question

How can you use what you know to help others?

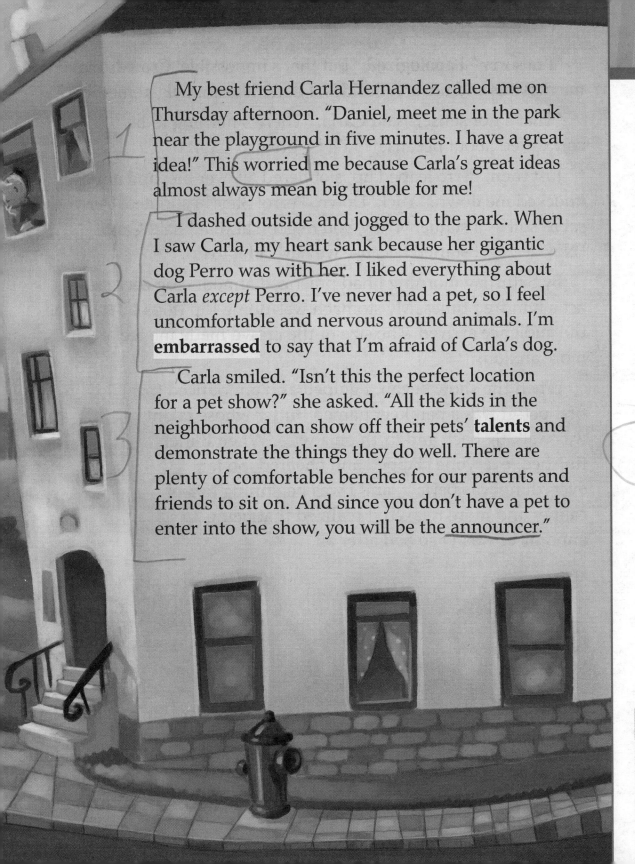

My best friend Carla Hernandez called me on Thursday afternoon. "Daniel, meet me in the park near the playground in five minutes. I have a great idea!" This worried me because Carla's great ideas almost always mean big trouble for me!

I dashed outside and jogged to the park. When I saw Carla, my heart sank because her gigantic dog Perro was with her. I liked everything about Carla *except* Perro. I've never had a pet, so I feel uncomfortable and nervous around animals. I'm **embarrassed** to say that I'm afraid of Carla's dog.

Carla smiled. "Isn't this the perfect location for a pet show?" she asked. "All the kids in the neighborhood can show off their pets' **talents** and demonstrate the things they do well. There are plenty of comfortable benches for our parents and friends to sit on. And since you don't have a pet to enter into the show, you will be the announcer."

FIND TEXT EVIDENCE 🔍

Read

Paragraph 1

Point of View

Circle the word that shows how Daniel feels about hearing Carla's great idea.

Paragraph 2

Ask and Answer Questions

Why isn't Daniel happy to see his best friend Carla? **Underline** text evidence to answer.

Paragraph 3

Dialogue

Why does Carla think Daniel should be the announcer?

Daniel dusint have a pet so Carla thinks Daniel can be a annoucer.

Draw a box around what Carla says.

Reread

Author's Craft

How does the author help you understand what the phrase "my heart sank" means?

SHARED READ

FIND TEXT EVIDENCE 🔍

Read

Paragraphs 1–5

Ask and Answer Questions

Think of a question about Carla or Daniel. Write it here.

Did Daniel think, this is impossible?

Underline text evidence that answers your question.

Paragraph 2

Prefixes

Find the word *nonsense*.

Circle the prefix. Use the prefix to figure out the meaning of the word.

It is not making sense

Reread

Author's Craft

How does the author help you understand how Daniel feels Saturday morning?

"I'm sorry," I **apologized**, "but that's impossible! Crowds make me nervous and unsure. Besides, I don't like animals, remember?"

"That's nonsense," said Carla. "There's nothing to be concerned about because you'll be great!"

Just then, Perro leaped up, slobbered all over me, and almost knocked me down. "Yuck. Down, Perro! Stay!" I shouted. Perro sat as still as a statue. "Wow, you're good at that," said Carla. "Now let's get started because we have a lot to do."

By Saturday morning I had practiced announcing each pet's act a hundred times. My stomach was doing flip flops by the time the **audience** arrived. The size of the crowd made me feel even more anxious.

When the show began, I gulped and announced the first pet. It was a parakeet named Butter whose talent was walking back and forth on a wire. When Butter finished, everyone clapped and cheered. So far, everything was perfect, and I was beginning to feel calmer and more relaxed. I **realized** that being an announcer wasn't so bad after all.

1 Then it was Carla and Perro's turn.

2 "Sit, Perro," she said, but Perro didn't sit.

3 Perro was not paying **attention** to Carla. He was too interested in watching Jack's bunnies jump in and out of their boxes. Suddenly, Perro leaped at the bunnies who hopped toward Mandy and knocked over her hamster's cage. Pudgy, the hamster, escaped and began running around in circles while Kyle's dog, Jake, howled. This was a disaster, and I had to do something.

4 "Sit!" I shouted at Perro. "Quiet!" I ordered Jake. "Stay!" I yelled. Everyone—kids and pets—stopped and stared at me. Even the audience froze.

5 "Daniel, that was incredible," said Carla. "You got the pets to settle down. That's quite an **achievement**."

6 Sadly, that was the end of our pet show. But now I have more **confidence** when I have to speak in front of people. And even though I am still nervous around animals, Perro and I have become great friends. And I've discovered my talent, too.

Marcin Piwowarski

Summarize

Use your notes and think about what happened in "The Impossible Pet Show." Summarize the important events. Talk about whether your prediction on page 104 was confirmed.

FIND TEXT EVIDENCE

Read
Paragraphs 1–4
Dialogue

Underline two things the characters say that real people might say.

Paragraphs 5–6
Point of View

How have Daniel's feelings about being an announcer changed?

Daniel feelings happy now,

 Circle text evidence that supports your answer.

Reread
Author's Craft

How does the author help you understand what talent Daniel has?

Vocabulary

Use the sentences to talk with a partner about each word. Then answer the questions.

achievement

It is a big **achievement** to fly a kite on a very windy day.

What is your biggest achievement?

X O do the backflip.

apologized

Kate **apologized** for breaking the dish.

When have you apologized for doing something?

I called my brother stide.

> **Build Your Word List** Reread page 106. Draw a box around a word you think is interesting. Use a dictionary to look up the word's meaning. Write the word and its definition in your writer's notebook.

attention

It is important to pay **attention** to directions.

How do you show your teacher you are paying attention in class?

by start staring o

audience

The **audience** clapped and cheered at the end of the play.

When have you been part of an audience?

never!

confidence

Jody read her report calmly and with **confidence**.

What does it mean to have confidence?

embarrassed

Tia was **embarrassed** when she forgot her lines in the play.

When have you felt embarrassed?

_____

_____

realized

My soccer team celebrated when we **realized** we had won the game.

Describe a time when you realized something.

_____

_____

talents

One of Lila's **talents** is playing the violin.

What is one of your talents?

_____

_____

Prefixes

A prefix is a word part added to the beginning of a word. A prefix changes the word's meaning. The prefixes *un-, non-,* and *im-* mean "not" or "opposite of."

🔍 **FIND TEXT EVIDENCE**

On page 106, I see the word unsure. *It has the root word* sure *and the prefix* un-. *I know that* sure *means "certain" and the prefix* un- *means "not." The word* unsure *must mean "not certain."*

Crowds make me nervous and unsure.

Your Turn Use the prefixes in each word to figure out its meaning.

uncomfortable, page 105 _____

impossible, page 106 _____

Ask and Answer Questions

Stop and ask yourself questions about "The Impossible Pet Show" as you read. Then look for story details to answer your questions. This can help you deepen your understanding of what you are reading.

FIND TEXT EVIDENCE

Look at page 105. Ask a question about what is happening. Then read again to find the answer.

Quick Tip

Asking questions helps you understand the text better. As you read, stop and ask yourself questions about the characters and what happens in the story. Then reread to find text evidence that answers your questions.

Page 105

I dashed outside and jogged to the park. When I saw Carla, my heart sank because her gigantic dog Perro was with her. I liked everything about Carla *except* Perro. I've never had a pet, so I feel uncomfortable and nervous around animals. I'm **embarrassed** to say that I'm afraid of Carla's dog.

Carla smiled. "Isn't this the perfect location for a pet show?" she asked. "All the kids in the neighborhood can show off their pets' **talents** and demonstrate the things they do well. There are plenty of comfortable benches for our parents and friends to sit on. And since you don't have a pet to enter into the show, you will be the announcer."

I don't understand why Carla's ideas are trouble for Daniel. <u>Daniel is uncomfortable around pets. Carla asks him to help at the pet show. Now I understand,</u> Carla's ideas are trouble for Daniel because she is asking Daniel to do something he is not comfortable doing.

Your Turn Reread "The Impossible Pet Show." Think of a question. You might ask: Why does Daniel think being an announcer isn't so bad? Reread page 106 to find the answer. Then write the answer here.

_____

_____

Dialogue and Illustrations

"The Impossible Pet Show" is **realistic fiction**. Realistic fiction

- is a made-up story that could really happen
- has dialogue and illustrations
- may be part of a longer book with chapters or part of a series about the same characters

🔍 FIND TEXT EVIDENCE

I can tell that "The Impossible Pet Show" is realistic fiction. The characters talk and act like real people. The events are made up, but they could really happen.

Page 106

"I'm sorry," I **apologized**, "but that's impossible! Crowds make me nervous and unsure. Besides, I don't like animals, remember?"

"That's nonsense," said Carla. "There's nothing to be concerned about because you'll be great!"

Just then, Perro leaped up, slobbered all over me, and almost knocked me down. "Yuck. Down, Perro! Stay!" I shouted. Perro sat as still as a statue. "Wow, you're good at that," said Carla. "Now let's get started because we have a lot to do."

By Saturday morning I had practiced announcing each pet's act a hundred times. My stomach was doing flip flops by the time the **audience** arrived. The size of the crowd made me feel even more anxious.

When the show began, I gulped and announced the first pet. It was a parakeet named Butter whose talent was walking back and forth on a wire. When Butter finished, everyone clapped and cheered. So far, everything was perfect, and I was beginning to feel calmer and more relaxed. I **realized** that being an announcer wasn't so bad after all.

Dialogue

Dialogue is what the characters say to each other.

Illustrations

Illustrations give more information or details about the characters and setting of the story.

Your Turn Reread page 105. Find two events that help you figure out this is realistic fiction. Write your answer below.

_____

_____

_____

Reread the dialogue on page 106. How does it help you understand the characters?

When you write realistic fiction, think about how you can use dialogue to show how each character feels.

Point of View

Point of view is what a narrator thinks about other characters or events in a story. Point of view also helps readers understand the relationship between the major and minor characters. Look for details that show what the narrator thinks. Use them to figure out the point of view.

🔍 FIND TEXT EVIDENCE

I read on page 105 that animals make Daniel nervous and uncomfortable. This will help me figure out what Daniel's point of view is about being an announcer for the pet show.

Quick Tip

Daniel is a major, or main, character in "The Impossible Pet Show." Jack is a minor character. To understand their relationship, think about what they say to each other. Think about what they do.

Details
Daniel says he is uncomfortable and nervous around animals.

↓

Point of View

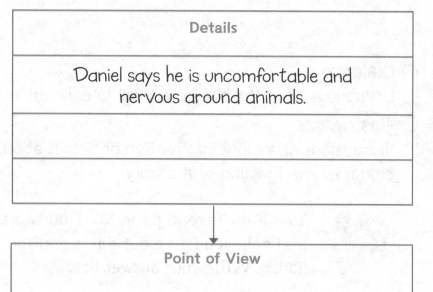

Your Turn Reread "The Impossible Pet Show." Find more details that tell what Daniel first thinks about being an announcer. List them in the graphic organizer. What is his point of view?

Details

Point of View

Respond to Reading

COLLABORATE

Talk about the prompt below. Think about how Daniel feels about being the announcer at the pet show. Use your notes and graphic organizer.

How does the author help you understand how Daniel changes from the beginning of the story to the end?

_____

_____

_____

_____

_____

_____

_____

_____

_____

_____

Quick Tip

Use these sentence starters to talk about how Daniel changes.

In the beginning, Daniel feels ...

I read that he ...

At the end, Daniel feels ...

Grammar Connections

As you write your response, be sure to use both simple and compound sentences. Use coordinating conjunctions to form compound subjects, predicates, and sentences.

Citing Sources

When you do research, you look at many different sources. They may be print or digital. Information from a source is someone else's work. It is important to list your sources on a page called **Works Cited**. Include these details when you cite your sources for a print book.

| Author | Title | City | Publisher | Type of source |

Baxter, Barry. *The History of Board Games*. Denver: Checkers Press, 2014. Print

Publication year

Include these details when you cite an online encyclopedia.

| Article title | Encyclopedia name | Publisher |

"Ancient Board Games." *Encyclopedia of Games Online*. Bonus Point Publications, 2011. Web. Feb. 11, 2015.

Publication year | Type of source | Date read online

Look at the box. What book did Megan use?

_____

What is the online encyclopedia article she cites?

_____

Write a Blog Talk with a partner about your talent. Use three sources to research the talent. Write a blog about it. Create a works cited page.

Works Cited

"Ancient Board Games." *Encyclopedia of Games Online*. Bonus Point Publications, 2011. Web. Feb. 11, 2015.

Baxter, Barry. *The History of Board Games*. Denver: Checkers Press, 2014. Print

This is what Megan's Works Cited page looks like.

The Talented Clementine

Literature Anthology:
pages 278–295

? How does the author help you understand how Margaret's teacher and Mrs. Rice are different?

Talk About It Reread paragraphs 3 and 4 on page 284. Turn to your partner and talk about what Margaret's teacher and Mrs. Rice do.

Cite Text Evidence What do Margaret's teacher and Mrs. Rice do and say that show how they are different? Write text evidence here.

 Make Inferences

Use text evidence and what you know to make an educated guess about how Margaret's teacher and Mrs. Rice feel about Clementine. What does it mean if someone gives a thumbs up?

Clues	How They Are Different

Write I know that Margaret's teacher and Mrs. Rice are different

_____

_____

How does the author use humor to describe how important Clementine is to the talent show?

Talk About It Reread page 291. Talk about how Clementine describes what's happening on stage.

Cite Text Evidence What words and phrases show that what happens is funny? Write evidence and tell how that helps you see how important Clementine is to the show.

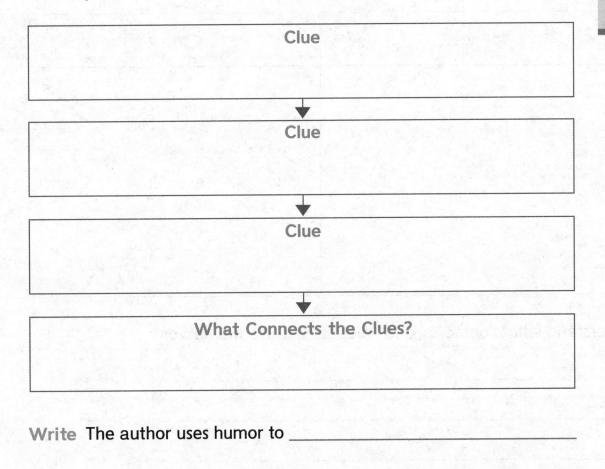

Clue

Clue

Clue

What Connects the Clues?

Write The author uses humor to _____

_____

How does the author help you understand what Principal Rice means when she tells Clementine that she is "one of a kind"?

Talk About It Reread the last two paragraphs on page 294. Talk about what Principal Rice says to Clementine and how it makes her feel.

Cite Text Evidence What clues help you understand what "one of a kind" means? Write text evidence in the chart.

Text Evidence	How It Helps

Write I understand what "one of a kind" means because the author

_____

_____

_____

Respond to Reading

COLLABORATE

Think about the author's descriptions of the characters and the events in the story. Use your notes and graphic organizer.

How does the author use what the characters do and say to help you understand how Clementine has changed?

_____

_____

_____

_____

_____

_____

_____

_____

_____

_____

_____

Quick Tip

Use these sentence starters to talk about Clementine.

At first, the author describes Clementine as ...

The author uses dialogue to tell me that Clementine's teachers think ...

I see how Clementine has changed because the author says ...

Self-Selected Reading

Choose a text. Read the first two pages. If five or more words are unfamiliar, pick another text. Fill in your writer's notebook with the title, author, genre, and your purpose for reading.

Clementine and the Family Meeting

? How does the author help you understand how Clementine feels about the family meeting?

Literature Anthology: pages 298–303

Talk About It Reread page 299. Discuss with a partner why you think Clementine is nervous about the family meeting.

Cite Text Evidence What words and phrases help you understand how Clementine feels? Write text evidence in the chart.

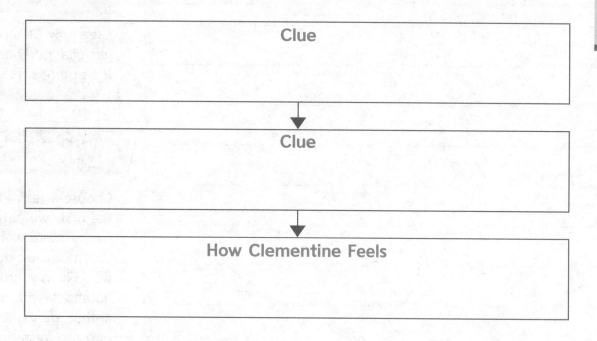

Clue

↓

Clue

↓

How Clementine Feels

Write The author helps me understand how Clementine feels by

_____

_____

? **How does the author use illustrations to help you understand how Clementine feels?**

COLLABORATE

Talk About It Look at the illustration on page 301. Turn to a partner and talk about what it shows you about how Clementine feels.

Cite Text Evidence What clues in the illustration help you understand how Clementine feels? Write them here.

Clues	How Clementine Feels

Write The illustration helps me understand how Clementine feels

_____

_____

_____

Quick Tip

I can use these sentence starters when we talk about the illustration.

The illustration shows Clementine . . .

This helps me understand that she feels . . .

? How do you know how Clementine feels about having a new baby in the family?

Talk About It Reread paragraph 3 on page 302. Talk about what Clementine says.

Cite Text Evidence What words and phrases help you know how she feels about having a new baby in the family? Write them here.

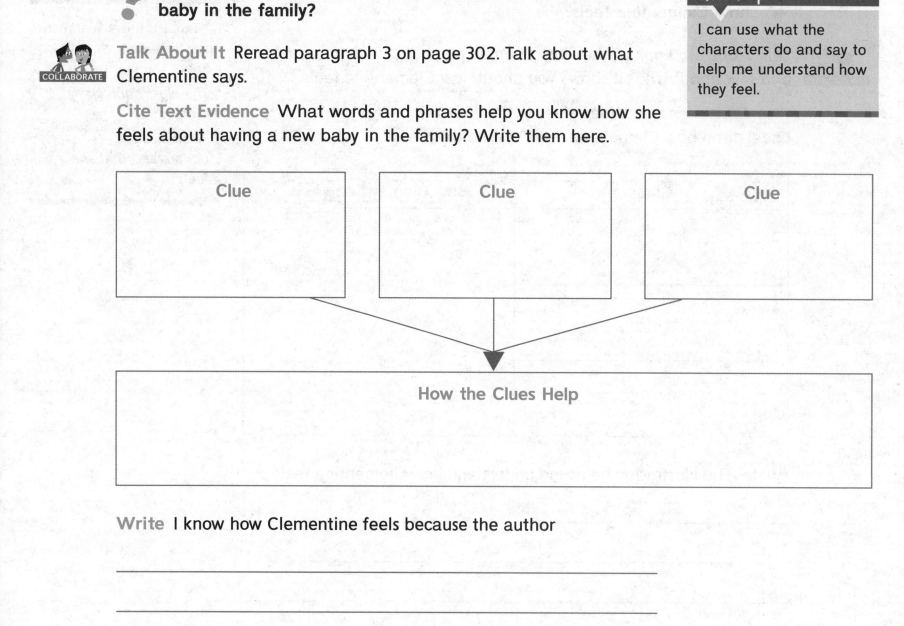

| Clue | Clue | Clue |

How the Clues Help

Write I know how Clementine feels because the author

_____

_____

_____

Figurative Language

Readers to Writers

Writers use figurative language to make their descriptions more interesting. Figurative language is any words or phrases that have a meaning that is different from the words' literal meaning. One kind of figurative language is a *simile*. A simile compares two things that are very different. Similes always have the words *like* or *as*.

Use the word *like* or *as* to compare a character to someone or something else. This kind of comparison, called a *simile*, can add interest and, in some cases, humor to your writing.

 FIND TEXT EVIDENCE

On page 302 of "Clementine and the Family Meeting" in the **Literature Anthology,** *the author describes Clementine's little brother as "a personal-size tornado." I know that her brother isn't really a small-sized tornado. The author uses a simile to compare the boy to a tornado because of the noise and the mess he is making by throwing all the pots and pans on the floor.*

COLLABORATE

Your Turn Reread page 303. What does the phrase "tornadoed kitchen" make you picture in your mind?

_____

_____

How does the author's use of figurative language help you picture what the kitchen looks like?

_____

_____

Text Connections

? **How do the photographer and the author of *The Talented Clementine* show how you can use what you know to help others?**

Talk About It Look at the photograph and read the caption. With a partner, talk about what the girls are doing.

Cite Text Evidence Circle details in the photograph that show what each girl's talent is. Then underline the text evidence in the caption that tells what they are doing. In the margin next to the photograph, tell how the girls feel. Underline evidence in the photograph that supports your answer.

Write The photographer and the

author help me understand _____

_____

_____

_____

_____

_____

Janey and Lucretia practice one hour a day. They are performing in a talent show and want to win.

Present Your Work

COLLABORATE

Decide how you will present your blog and illustration to the class. If possible, project your text and image on a whiteboard for your audience. Also display your works cited page to show your list of sources. Use the checklist to improve your presentation.

Bree's Blog About Bees

I'm Bree, and I love bees. My mom is a beekeeper, and we sell honey. I've learned a lot about bees. This blog is to share what I know. Today's topic: Stay safe around bees.

The most interesting thing I learned about my talent is: _____

_____

One thing I would like to learn more about is _____.

I think my presentation was _____.

Quick Tip

Be sure to practice reading your blog several times before you present it. Identify any words, such as names or multisyllabic words, that might be difficult to pronounce. Slow down when you get to these words and focus on reading them accurately.

✓ Presenting Checklist

☐ I will practice my presentation.

☐ I will make eye contact with the audience.

☐ I will speak clearly and at an appropriate speed.

☐ I will include a works cited page for my sources.

☐ I will pause at the end and ask if my audience has any questions.

Literature Anthology: pages 278–295

Expert Model

Features of Realistic Fiction

In realistic fiction stories, the characters talk and act like real people. They include events that could happen in real life. Realistic fiction

- is a made-up story that could really happen
- has a beginning, middle, and end
- has dialogue and illustrations

Word Wise

On page 280, Sara Pennypacker tells about what is happening to Clementine. This helps us understand how she feels. Marla Frazee's illustration helps us see how Clementine feels, too.

Analyze an Expert Model A good way to learn how to write a realistic fiction story is to read one. Reread the first two paragraphs on page 280 of *The Talented Clementine* in the **Literature Anthology**. Use text evidence to answer the questions.

How do you know this is realistic fiction?

_____

_____

How does the author help you understand how Clementine feels at the beginning of the story?

_____

_____

_____

Plan: Choose Your Topic

COLLABORATE

Mapping With a partner, think of one or more characters you have read about who use their talents to help others. When you write a realistic fiction story, your character should have talents that real people have. Use the sentence starters below to discuss your ideas.

I read about a character who . . .

This character's talent is . . .

He/she uses that talent to . . .

Writing Prompt Choose from your ideas to write a realistic fiction story about a character who uses a talent to help others.

I will write about _____.

Purpose and Audience An author's purpose is the main reason for writing. Your audience is who will be reading it.

What is your purpose for writing your story? _____

_____

Who will read your realistic fiction story? _____

_____

Plan In your writer's notebook, make a Sequence chart to plan your writing. Fill in the characters, setting, and the first event, or how you want the story to start.

> **Quick Tip**
>
> Mapping is a way to plan your writing. It can help you figure out the setting and plot of a story. It can also help you create realistic characters. Use a graphic organizer to write down your ideas. Then use your ideas to write your story. A Sequence chart is a good tool for mapping a story and its characters.

Character

Setting

Beginning
↓
| Middle |
↓
| End |

Plan: Sequence

Sequence of Events Writers tell the events of a story in order. These events become the story's plot. Characters often have a problem to solve. How they solve the problem are the plot events.

In "The Impossible Pet Show," Daniel has a problem. Reread to see how the author tells what happens in order to describe the problem.

> Suddenly, Perro leaped at the bunnies who hopped toward Mandy and knocked over her hamster's cage. Pudgy, the hamster, escaped and began running around in circles while Kyle's dog, Jake, howled.
>
> "Sit!" I shouted at Perro. "Quiet!" I ordered Jake. "Stay!" I yelled.

How does the author help you understand Daniel's problem?

_____

_____

Now think about your character. What is your character's problem?

_____

_____

Sequence Chart In your writer's notebook, fill in the important events in your Sequence chart.

Draft

Dialogue Dialogue is the actual words that characters in a story speak. It is used to show how different characters communicate with each other. Dialogue can show a character's response to situations, their feelings and emotions, or their thoughts about events in the story. Reread this excerpt from "Painting From Memory." The author uses dialogue to show how the characters feel.

> I lived in Damyang until last year. My family moved to New York because my mother is a scientist and she was asked to come here to work.
>
> "Jae," she said, "you'll like New York."
>
> I was unsure. "I'll like nothing there. I'll miss home," I said.

Now use the above dialogue as a model to write what your characters might say to each other.

_____

_____

_____

Write a Draft Look over your Sequence chart. Use it to help you write your draft in your writer's notebook. Remember to put story events in order and to include dialogue between the characters.

Revise

Signal Words Writers use signal words to help readers understand the sequence of events. Signal words also help to connect the parts of a story. Words like *first, next, then,* and *last* help the reader figure out the order of events.

Reread page 290 of *The Talented Clementine* in the **Literature Anthology**. Talk with a partner about how the author uses signal words to show the sequence of events. Write about it here.

_____

_____

_____

Revise It's time to revise your writing. Read your draft and look for places where you might

- add signal words

- put the events in the correct order

Circle two sentences in your draft that you can change. Revise and write them here.

 1 _____

 2 _____

_____

Peer Conferences

COLLABORATE

Review a Draft Listen carefully as a partner reads his or her draft aloud. Tell what you like about the draft. Use these sentence starters to help you discuss your partner's draft.

I like this part because ...

Add more dialogue here to explain ...

Use more signal words to show ...

I have a question about ...

Partner Feedback After you take turns giving each other feedback, write one of the suggestions from your partner that you will use in your revision.

_____

_____

_____

_____

_____

Revision After you finish your peer conference, use the Revising Checklist to help you figure out what you can change to make your realistic fiction story better. Remember to use the rubric on page 133 to help you with your revision.

✓ Revising Checklist

☐ Are the events of my realistic fiction story in order?

☐ Do I use signal words to connect the events of the story?

☐ Is there a beginning, middle, and end?

☐ Does my dialogue sound the way real people talk?

☐ Did I include illustrations in my story?

Edit and Proofread

After you revise your realistic fiction story, proofread it to find any mistakes in grammar, spelling, and punctuation. Read your draft at least three times. This will help you catch any mistakes. Use the checklist below to edit your sentences.

✓ Editing Checklist

☐ Do all sentences begin with a capital letter and end with a punctuation mark?

☐ Are linking verbs used when appropriate?

☐ Are quotation marks used correctly in dialogue?

☐ Are all words spelled correctly?

List two mistakes that you found as you proofread your realistic fiction story.

1 _____

_____

_____

2 _____

_____

_____

Grammar Connections

When you proofread your draft for mistakes, remember to look for places where linking words such as *am, is, was,* or *were* can be used to connect subjects with more information that describes that subject, as in "In class, she *was* very quiet, but on stage, she *was* loud and outgoing."

Publish, Present, and Evaluate

Publishing When you publish your writing, you create a neat final copy that is free of mistakes. Be sure to print neatly. Leave the space of a pencil point between letters and the space of the width of a pencil between words.

Presentation When you are ready to present, practice your presentation. Use the presenting checklist.

Evaluate After you publish, use the rubric to evaluate it.

1 Which parts of your story are you proud of? _____

_____

2 What might need more work? _____

_____

4	3	2	1
• all events are in sequential order • several signal words are used • dialogue and illustrations are used throughout the story	• most events are in sequential order • some signal words are used • dialogue and illustrations are used in most of the story	• some events are out of order • a few signal words are used • dialogue and illustrations are used in part of the story	• events are out of order and hard to follow • signal words are not used • dialogue and illustrations are not used

Essential Question

How do animals adapt to challenges in their habitat?

This ermine's fur is brown and white in summer. It turns white in winter to blend in with the snow. This adaptation helps the ermine escape its predators. Ermines are also fast runners and good climbers. They have an excellent sense of smell, too.

Look at the photograph. Talk about how the ermine's adaptations help it survive. Remember to follow agreed upon discussion rules.

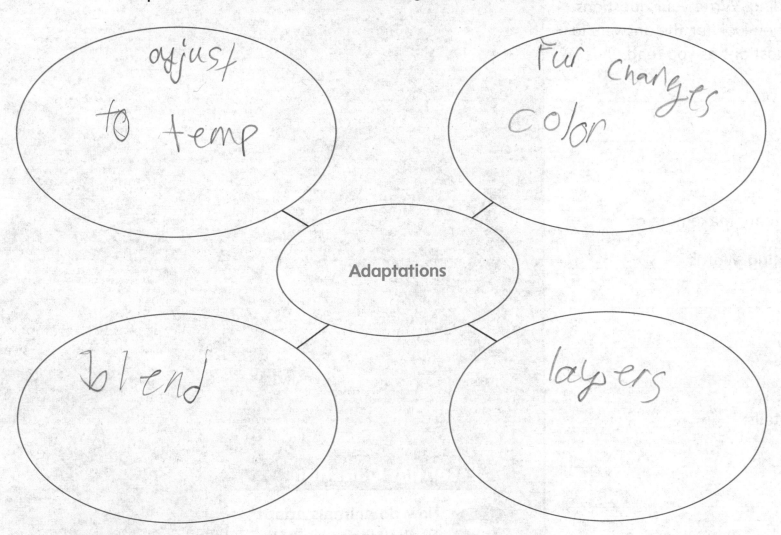

adjust to temp

Fur changes color

Adaptations

blend

layers

Go online to **my.mheducation.com** and read the "Creatures of the Deep" Blast. Think about what strange animals live in the deepest parts of the ocean. Then blast back your response.

TAKE NOTES

Asking questions before you read helps you figure out your purpose for reading. Write your questions here. Then look for the answers to your questions as you read.

What do they do.

As you read, make note of:

Interesting Words: _____

_____

_____

_____

Key Details: _____

_____

_____

_____

_____

GRAY WOLF! RED FOX!

Essential Question

? How do animals adapt to challenges in their habitat?

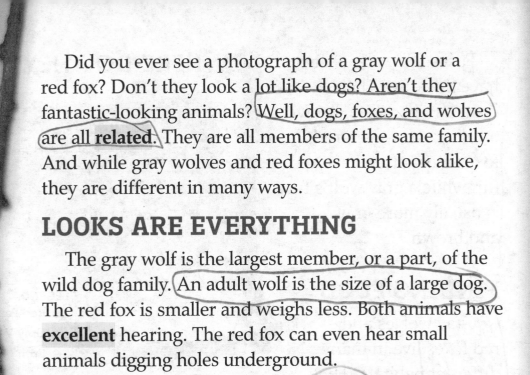

Did you ever see a photograph of a gray wolf or a red fox? Don't they look a lot like dogs? Aren't they fantastic-looking animals? Well, dogs, foxes, and wolves are all **related**. They are all members of the same family. And while gray wolves and red foxes might look alike, they are different in many ways.

LOOKS ARE EVERYTHING

The gray wolf is the largest member, or a part, of the wild dog family. An adult wolf is the size of a large dog. The red fox is smaller and weighs less. Both animals have **excellent** hearing. The red fox can even hear small animals digging holes underground.

And just take a look at those beautiful tails! The gray wolf and red fox both have long, bushy tails. The wolf's tail can be two feet long. The fox's tail is not as long but has a bright, white tip. In the winter, foxes use their thick, furry tails as **protection** from the cold.

The gray wolf and red fox are both mammals.

EXPOSITORY TEXT

FIND TEXT EVIDENCE

Read

Paragraph 1

Reread

What animals are foxes related to?

dog ans wolves

Draw a box around text evidence to support your answer.

Paragraphs 2–3

Compare and Contrast

How is the gray wolf like a dog? **Underline** text evidence.

Captions

What new information did you learn about the gray wolf and red fox in the caption?

both are mammals

Reread

Author's Craft

Why is "Looks Are Everything" a good heading for this section?

SHARED READ

FIND TEXT EVIDENCE 🔍

Read

Maps

Use the legend, or key. **Circle** places on the map where both red foxes and gray wolves live.

Paragraph 1

Compare and Contrast

Underline how a wolf's fur and a fox's fur are the same.

Paragraph 2

Sentence Clues

Draw a box around clues that tell what *habitats* are.

Paragraph 3

Reread

Why don't foxes and wolves compete for food? Write it here.

They have diffient diets.

Reread

Author's Craft

How does the author use words and phrases to help you visualize what red foxes do to get food?

Foxes and wolves also have thick fur. Their coats can be white, brown, or black. However, red foxes most often have red fur, while a gray wolf's fur is usually more gray and brown.

FINDING FOOD

Gray wolves and red foxes live in many different habitats. They live in forests, deserts, woodlands, and grasslands. But as more people build roads and shopping centers, both animals have lost their homes. The red fox has adapted well, or made changes to fit into its **environment**. Now more foxes make their homes close to towns and parks. Wolves, however, stay far away from towns and people.

Foxes and wolves are not in **competition** for food. They have different diets. Red foxes **prefer** to hunt alone and eat small animals, birds, and fish. They also like to raid garbage cans and campsites for food. Wolves work together in packs, or groups, to hunt large animals, such as moose and deer.

WHERE DO THEY LIVE?

LEGEND
- Red Fox only
- Gray Wolf only
- Both

Gray wolves prefer to live and hunt in packs.

DAY-TO-DAY

Wolves live in packs of four to seven. They do almost everything together. They hunt, travel, and choose safe places to set up dens for **shelter**. Foxes, on the other hand, like to live alone. They usually sleep in the open or find an empty hole to call home.

The red fox hunts for food alone.

Both wolves and foxes communicate by barking and growling. The gray wolf also howls to **alert**, or warn, other wolves when there is danger nearby. The red fox signals in a different way. It waves its tail in the air to caution other foxes.

The gray wolf and red fox are members of the same family and have many things in common. But they really are two very different animals.

Summarize

Use your notes and think about the comparisons made in "Gray Wolf! Red Fox!" Summarize the important similarities and differences.

FIND TEXT EVIDENCE

Read

Paragraph 1

Compare and Contrast

Underline text evidence that shows what's different about where wolves and foxes live.

Paragraphs 2–3

Sentence Clues

What clues help you figure out what *signals* means?

Danger!

Reread

Author's Craft

How do you know how the author feels about the gray wolf and the red fox?

Fluency

Take turns reading the last two paragraphs. Think about the meaning of what you're reading to make sure you pronounce each word correctly.

Vocabulary

Use the sentences to talk with a partner about each word. Then answer the questions.

alert

Wolves howl to **alert** other wolves when danger is nearby.

How would you alert someone to talk quietly?

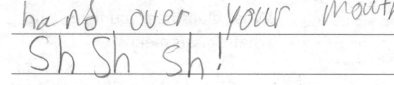

hand over your mouth!
Sh sh sh!

competition

Nathan won the **competition** because he was the fastest runner.

What kind of competition have you participated in?

_____

_____

> **Build Your Word List** Reread paragraph 3 on page 137. Draw a box around the word *protection*. In your writer's notebook, use a word web to write more forms of the word. Use a dictionary to help you.

environment

The polar bear lives in a cold and snowy **environment**.

Describe a whale's environment.

_____

_____

excellent

Lily's **excellent** artwork won first place in the art show.

Describe something you did that was excellent.

_____

_____

prefer

Andre and his friends **prefer** walking to riding their bikes.

What kind of transportation do you prefer?

_____

_____

protection

The skunk's scent provides **protection** from its enemies.

What do you use for protection on sunny days?

_____

_____

related

Josh and Jen are **related** because they are both members of the same family.

What two animals are related?

_____

_____

shelter

Our tent was a dry and safe **shelter** during the storm.

What is another kind of shelter people use?

_____

_____

Sentence Clues

Sentence clues are words or phrases in a sentence, or a nearby sentence, that help you figure out the meaning of an unfamiliar word. Sometimes clues define, or tell exactly, what a word means.

FIND TEXT EVIDENCE

I'm not sure what the word member *means on page 137. I see the words "a part of" in the same sentence. This clue tells me that* member *means "a part of something."*

The gray wolf is the largest member, or a part, of the wild dog family.

Your Turn Find context clues to figure out the meanings of these words.

adapted, page 138 _____

packs, page 138 _____

Talk about the sentence clues that helped you figure out the meanings.

Reread

Stop and think about the text as you read. Are there new facts and ideas? Do they make sense? Reread to make sure you understand.

🔍 FIND TEXT EVIDENCE

Do you understand how fox fur is like wolf fur? Reread the first paragraph on page 138.

Page 138

Foxes and wolves also have thick fur. Their coats can be white, brown, or black. However, red foxes most often have red fur, while a gray wolf's fur is usually more gray and brown.

WHERE

I read that foxes and wolves both have thick fur. I also read that their coats can be white, brown, or black. Now I understand some of the ways fox fur is like wolf fur.

Your Turn Reread "Day-to-Day" on page 139. Do you understand the difference between how wolves and foxes communicate? With a partner, find text evidence about how wolves and foxes communicate in different ways. Then write the answer here.

_____

_____

Maps and Captions

"Gray Wolf! Red Fox!" is an **expository text**. Expository texts

- give facts and information to explain a topic
- may be about science topics
- include text features such as a map, photographs, and captions

🔍 FIND TEXT EVIDENCE

I can tell that "Gray Wolf! Red Fox!" is an expository text. It explains how gray wolves and red foxes are alike and different. It includes a map, photographs, and captions.

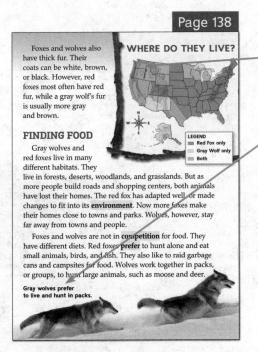

Page 138

Foxes and wolves also have thick fur. Their coats can be white, brown, or black. However, red foxes most often have red fur, while a gray wolf's fur is usually more gray and brown.

WHERE DO THEY LIVE?

LEGEND
- Red Fox only
- Gray Wolf only
- Both

FINDING FOOD

Gray wolves and red foxes live in many different habitats. They live in forests, deserts, woodlands, and grasslands. But as more people build roads and shopping centers, both animals have lost their homes. The red fox has adapted well, or made changes to fit into its **environment**. Now more foxes make their homes close to towns and parks. Wolves, however, stay far away from towns and people.

Foxes and wolves are not in **competition** for food. They have different diets. Red foxes **prefer** to hunt alone and eat small animals, birds, and fish. They also like to raid garbage cans and campsites for food. Wolves work together in packs, or groups, to hunt large animals, such as moose and deer.

Gray wolves prefer to live and hunt in packs.

Map

A map is a flat drawing of a place. It has a legend that shows what colors and symbols mean.

Caption

A caption explains a photograph or illustration. It sometimes gives more information about a topic.

COLLABORATE

Your Turn Look at the text features in "Gray Wolf! Red Fox!" Tell your partner about something you learned using the text features. Write your answer below.

_____

_____

_____

Compare and Contrast

Authors use compare and contrast to help you understand more about two things. When authors compare, they show how two things are alike. When they contrast, they tell how two things are different.

🔍 FIND TEXT EVIDENCE

How are red foxes and gray wolves alike? How are they different? I will reread paragraph 2 on page 137 of "Gray Wolf! Red Fox!" to find out.

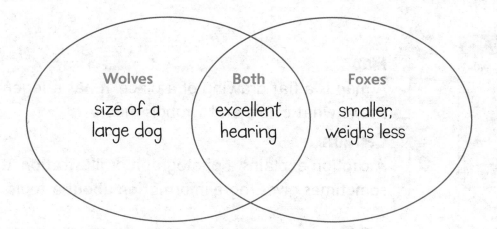

Wolves	Both	Foxes
size of a large dog	excellent hearing	smaller, weighs less

Your Turn Reread "Finding Food" on page 138. Find details that tell how red foxes and gray wolves are alike and different. Add these details to your graphic organizer.

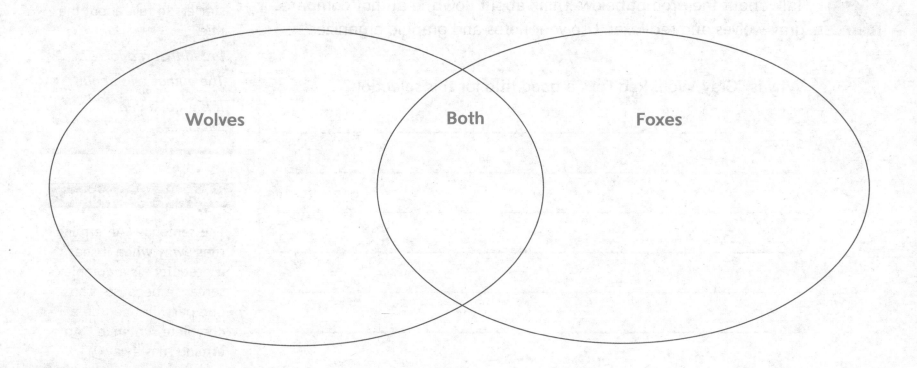

Wolves

Both

Foxes

Respond to Reading

COLLABORATE

Talk about the prompt below. Think about how the author compares gray wolves and red foxes. Use your notes and graphic organizer.

Why is "Gray Wolf! Red Fox!" a good title for this selection?

_____

_____

_____

_____

_____

_____

_____

_____

_____

_____

_____

_____

Find Relevant Information

Finding relevant information means searching a variety of sources to identify and gather research on a topic. Some examples of sources include

- encyclopedias and dictionaries
- books
- magazine articles
- photographs and maps
- reliable websites

It is important to find information that is relevant or related to your topic. Think about an animal that lives near you. Where can you find information about what it looks like, where it lives, and how it finds food?

Look at the checklist of sources. Make a check mark next to three sources you think would be good resources to find relevant information.

 Make a Collage A collage is a poster with photographs, maps, and facts. With a partner, research the animal you chose. Collect information about what the animal looks like, how it finds food, and where it lives. Use these steps to create your collage:

1. Find and gather relevant information from a variety of sources.
2. Note facts and collect photographs.
3. Organize your research. Add photographs, illustrations, facts, captions, and maps to create your collage.

Discuss your sources with a partner. Talk about how you know the information you found is relevant. Remember to converse politely.

☐ Encyclopedias and dictionaries
☐ Books
☐ Magazine articles
☐ Photographs and maps
☐ Reliable websites

Amazing Wildlife of the Mojave

 How does the author use words and phrases to help you visualize how the chuckwalla protects itself?

Literature Anthology: pages 304–315

COLLABORATE

Talk About It Reread page 307. Talk with a partner about how the chuckwalla protects itself.

Cite Text Evidence What words does the author use to describe what the chuckwalla does to protect itself? Write text evidence in the chart.

Make Inferences

An inference is a guess you make based on what you know. Make an inference about how the author feels about how the chuckwalla protects itself. Find text evidence to support your inference.

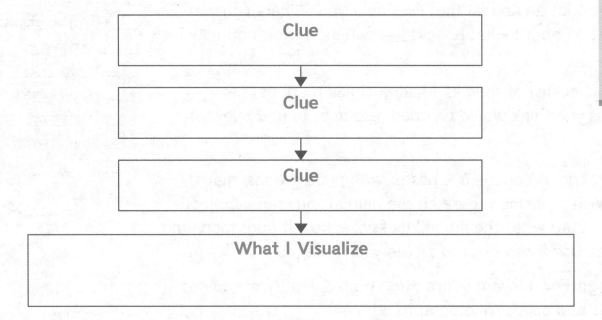

```
┌─────────────────────┐
│        Clue         │
└─────────────────────┘
           ↓
┌─────────────────────┐
│        Clue         │
└─────────────────────┘
           ↓
┌─────────────────────┐
│        Clue         │
└─────────────────────┘
           ↓
┌─────────────────────────────┐
│     What I Visualize        │
└─────────────────────────────┘
```

Write I can visualize how the chuckwalla protects itself because

_____

_____

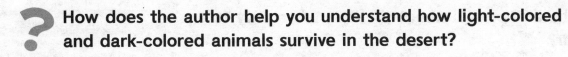

? How does the author help you understand how light-colored and dark-colored animals survive in the desert?

Talk About It Reread page 309. Talk with a partner about why "Light Colors Help" is a good heading for this section.

Cite Text Evidence What text evidence shows how animals survive in the Mojave Desert? Write it in the chart.

Light-colored animals	Dark-colored animals

Write The author helps me understand how light-colored and

dark-colored animals survive by _____

_____

_____

Quick Tip

I can use these sentence starters to talk to my partner about animals in the desert.

In this section, the author describes...

It helps me understand that animals...

Evaluate Information

Notice the image at the top of page 309. How does it help readers better understand why light colors are an advantage in the desert?

? **How does the author feel about the iguana's ability to change color?**

Talk About It Reread the second paragraph on page 314. Talk with a partner about how the author describes what iguanas do.

Cite Text Evidence What clues help you see how the author feels about what iguanas can do? Write evidence to support your answer.

Text Evidence	How the Author Feels

Write I know how the author feels about iguanas because _____

_____

_____

Respond to Reading

Talk about the prompt below. Think about how the author's words, phrases, and punctuation reflect his point of view about the desert and desert animals. Use your notes and graphic organizer.

How do you know how the author feels about the wildlife in the Mojave?

_____

_____

_____

_____

_____

_____

_____

_____

Quick Tip

Use these sentence starters to talk about how the author feels about wildlife in the Mojave.

The author says that living in the desert is...

He tells about how the animals...

This helps me know that he feels...

Self-Selected Reading

Choose a text. In your writer's notebook, write the title, author, and genre of the book. As you read, make a connection to ideas in other texts you have read or to a personal experience. Write your ideas in your notebook.

Little Half Chick

1   Once in Mexico, an unusual chick hatched. He had only one eye, one wing, and one leg. He was named Little Half Chick. He quickly learned to hop faster on one leg than most chickens could walk on two. He was a curious and adventurous chick and soon grew tired of his barnyard environment. One day he decided to hop to Mexico City to meet the mayor.

2   Along the way, he hopped by a stream blocked with weeds. "Could you clear these weeds away so my water can run freely?" the stream gurgled. Little Half Chick helped the stream. Then he hopped on.

3   It started to rain. A small fire on the side of the road crackled, "Please give me shelter from this rain, or I will go out!" Little Half Chick stretched out his wing to protect the fire until the rain stopped.

Literature Anthology:
pages 318–319

Reread and use the prompts to take notes in the text.

In the first paragraph, **circle** words and phrases that describe Little Half Chick. Write them here:

_____

_____

_____

COLLABORATE

Reread paragraphs 2 and 3. Talk with a partner about what Little Half Chick does to help the stream and the fire. **Underline** text evidence.

4   Further down the road Little Half Chick met a wind that was tangled in a prickly bush. "Please untangle me," it whispered. Little Half Chick untangled the wind. Then he hopped on to Mexico City.

5   Little Half Chick did not meet the mayor. He met the mayor's cook. She grabbed him, plunged him into a pot of water, and lit a fire. However, the fire and the water remembered Little Half Chick's kindness. The fire refused to burn, and the water refused to boil. Then, the grateful wind picked him up and carried him safely to the top of the highest tower in Mexico City.

6   Little Half Chick became a weather vane. His flat body told everyone below the direction the wind blew. And he learned this lesson: Always help someone in need because you don't know when you'll need help.

Reread paragraph 4. **Circle** how Little Half Chick helps the wind.

COLLABORATE

Reread paragraphs 5 and 6. Talk with a partner about what happens to Little Half Chick when he meets the mayor's cook. **Underline** words and phrases that describe what happens.

How does Little Half Chick escape the pot of water? Make marks in the margin beside the text evidence. Write it here.

_____

_____

_____

_____

_____

_____

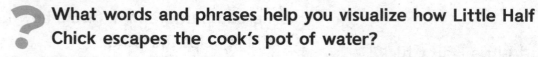

? **What words and phrases help you visualize how Little Half Chick escapes the cook's pot of water?**

Talk About It Reread paragraph 5 on page 153. Turn and talk with a partner about how Little Half Chick escapes.

Cite Text Evidence What words and phrases help you picture what happens? Write text evidence in the chart.

Clue

↓

Clue

↓

Clue

↓

I Visualize

Write The author helps me visualize how Little Half Chick escapes by

_____

_____

_____

Author's Message

Readers to Writers

An author often has a message or lesson that he or she wants the reader to learn from the text. Sometimes the author uses events in the story as clues to show his or her message.

FIND TEXT EVIDENCE

On page 153 of "Little Half Chick" in paragraph 6, the author states the message of the fable. The events in the story lead up to the lesson Little Half Chick learns.

Before writing, think about what you want your readers to learn. Write down the message you want to share with your readers. Then choose words and phrases that will be clues to help readers understand your message.

> Little Half Chick became a weather vane. His flat body told everyone below the direction the wind blew. And he learned this lesson: Always help someone in need because you don't know when you'll need help.

Your Turn Look back at your annotations in paragraphs 2 and 3 on page 152 of "Little Half Chick."

How does the author give clues to help you understand the fable's

message? _____

_____

Reread paragraph 5 on page 153. What words help you see that the fire, water, and wind are clues to the lesson Little Half Chick learns?

_____

Text Connections

? **How do this photograph and the photographs and illustrations in *Amazing Wildlife of the Mojave* and "Little Half Chick" help you understand how animals adapt to challenges?**

Talk About It Look at the photograph and read the caption. Talk with a partner about what you see.

Cite Text Evidence Circle the sea cucumber crab. Now draw a circle about the same size somewhere on the sea cucumber. Compare what's inside both circles. Think about how the authors in the texts you read use photographs and illustrations to help you understand more about the topic.

Write Photographs and illustrations help

me understand _____

_____

_____

_____

_____

_____

_____

Quick Tip

I see that the photographer is helping me understand how crabs protect themselves. This will help me compare the photograph to the text.

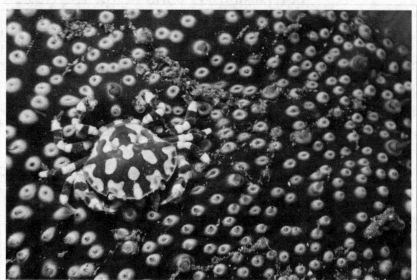

Do you see the sea cucumber crab? He's there. He's resting on a sea cucumber. These crabs use camouflage to protect themselves from animals that want to eat them.

Present Your Work

COLLABORATE

Decide how you will present your collage. Create a digital slideshow, or simply present the collage directly to your class. Use the checklist to help you improve your presentation.

Bears

Presenting Checklist

- [ ] I will practice the timing of my presentation.
- [ ] I will make sure people can see my presentation.
- [ ] I will make sure the text is big enough to read.
- [ ] I will spell-check my presentation.

Before I present, I will practice the timing of my presentation by:

_____.

I think the pace of my presentation was _____

_____.

I know because _____

_____.

Talk About It

Essential Question

How can others inspire us?

COLLABORATE

Danny talked to firefighters in his neighborhood. He learned what they do. Danny was inspired by these brave and helpful heroes. People who are courageous and helpful inspire us. When we feel inspired, we want to help others, too.

Look at the photograph. Talk with a partner about how other people are inspiring. Write words about inspiration in the web.

SOCIAL STUDIES

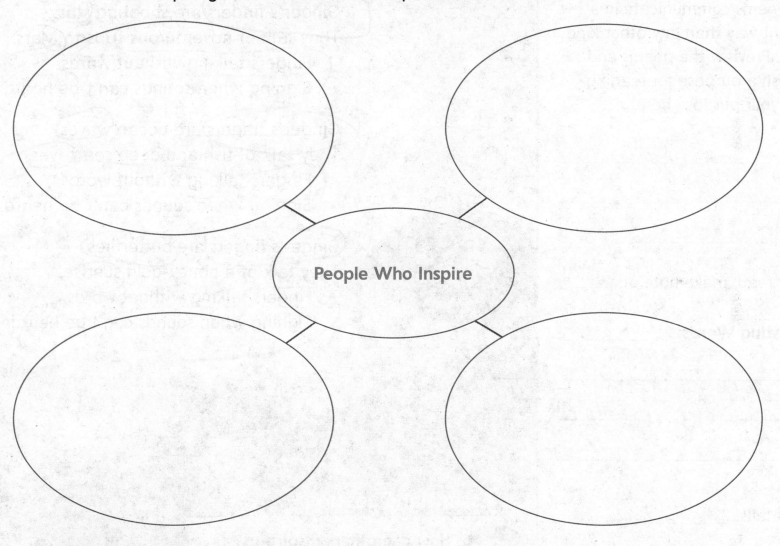

People Who Inspire

BLAST BACK!
studysync

Go online to **my.mheducation.com** and read the "An Inspirational Poet" Blast. Think about what inspired Phillis Wheatley. Then blast back your response.

TAKE NOTES

Understanding why you are reading helps you adjust how you read. Poems communicate in a different way than any other kind of text. Preview the poems and establish a purpose for reading. Write your purpose here.

_____

_____

_____

As you read, make note of:

Interesting Words: _____

_____

_____

_____

Key Details: _____

_____

_____

Ginger's Fingers

Ginger's fingers are shooting stars,
They talk of adventurous trips to Mars.
Fingers talking without words,
Signing when sounds can't be heard.

Ginger's fingers are ocean waves,
They talk of fish and deep sea caves.
Fingers talking without words,
Signing when sounds can't be heard.

Ginger's fingers are butterflies,
They talk of a honey-gold sunrise.
Fingers talking without words,
Signing when sounds can't be heard.

Essential Question

How can others inspire us?

Read about different ways that people inspire others.

The Giant

Dodge, dart, dash,
    Zigzag, slash!
I sizzle, SIZZLE, when I dribble,
I'm lightning on the court.
My team calls me The Giant,
Even though I'm kinda short.

The other team might laugh to see
A player tiny as a flea.

But I'm a rocket, fiery hot,
Watch me soar, SOAR, on my jump shot!

Stretching, flexing, push, push, PUSH,
My ball flies up and in —Swoosh Woosh!

I show them all
You don't need tall
To rule the ball!

FIND TEXT EVIDENCE

Read

Page 160

Rhyme

In the second stanza, **underline** two words that rhyme.

Page 160

Repetition

Draw a box around the lines that are repeated, or are the same, in all three stanzas.

Page 161

Metaphor

Circle a metaphor in the third stanza. What two things are being compared?

The kid and the rocket.

Reread

Author's Craft

Why is "The Giant" a good title for this poem?

`Read`

Page 162

Metaphor

Underline two metaphors in the first stanza.

Page 162

Repetition

Draw a box around the repetition in the second stanza. What does it help you visualize?

Thunder rumbled

Page 162

Theme

How does the crew feel in the last stanza?

The crew felt extremely terrified.

`Reread`

Author's Craft

How does the poet help you understand how the weather changes?

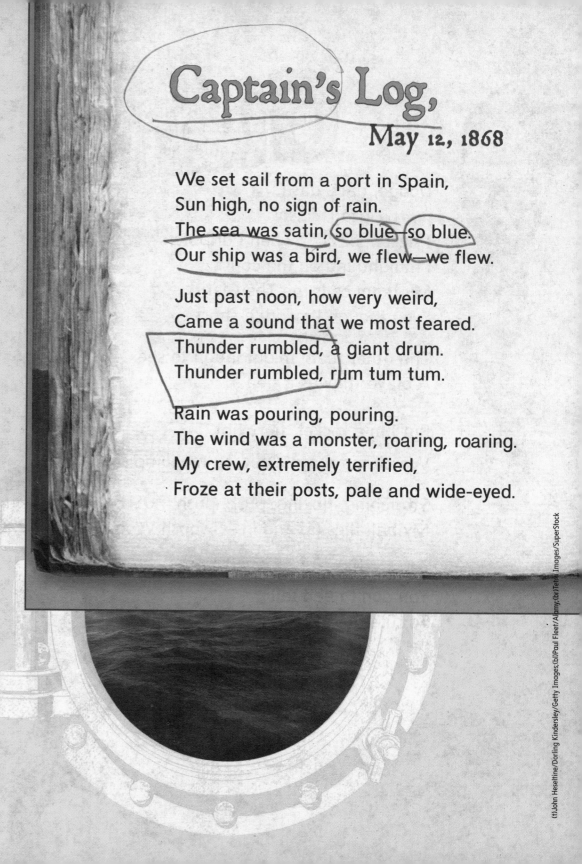

Captain's Log,
May 12, 1868

We set sail from a port in Spain,
Sun high, no sign of rain.
The sea was satin, so blue—so blue.
Our ship was a bird, we flew—we flew.

Just past noon, how very weird,
Came a sound that we most feared.
Thunder rumbled, a giant drum.
Thunder rumbled, rum tum tum.

Rain was pouring, pouring.
The wind was a monster, roaring, roaring.
My crew, extremely terrified,
Froze at their posts, pale and wide-eyed.

(t)John Heseltine/Dorling Kindersley/Getty Images;(b)Paul Fleet/Alamy;(br)Tetra Images/SuperStock

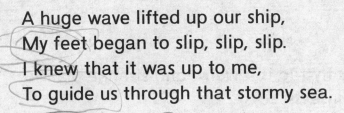

A huge wave lifted up our ship,
My feet began to slip, slip, slip.
I knew that it was up to me,
To guide us through that stormy sea.

I grabbed a rope, reached for the mast,
And got back to the helm at last—at last
Shook off the rain, looked at my crew,
"Steady lads, I'll get us through."

The crew heard my call,
Each lad stood up tall.
All hands now on deck, we trimmed every sail.
Courageous, together, we rode out that gale.

FIND TEXT EVIDENCE

Read

Page 163

Stanzas

Who is telling the story?

The captain

Circle text evidence in each stanza that supports your answer.

Page 163

Theme

What is the theme, or main message, of the poem?

The message is not to give up and don't fail your crew

Underline text evidence that supports your answer.

Reread

Author's Craft

How does the poet help you visualize how the captain inspires his crew?

Make Connections

Which character from the poems do you find most inspiring? Why?

Vocabulary

Use the example sentences to talk with a partner about each word. Then answer the questions.

adventurous

You must be **adventurous** to try whitewater rafting.

What else do you have to be adventurous to try?

_____

_____

courageous

The **courageous** firefighter rescued people from a burning building.

Describe another person who is courageous.

_____

_____

extremely

Cactuses can grow in **extremely** dry places.

Describe a time when you were extremely cold.

_____

_____

weird

The Venus flytrap is a **weird** and strange plant that eats insects.

What is a synonym for weird?

_____

_____

Poetry Terms

free verse

Some of Emma's **free verse** poems rhyme, and some do not.

What rule don't free verse poems have to follow?

_____

_____

narrative poem

I wrote a **narrative poem** about the American Revolution.

What would you like to write a narrative poem about?

_____

_____

repetition

Repeating words or phrases to create rhythm is called **repetition**.

Name one effect of using repetition.

_____

_____

rhyme

The words *night* and *right* **rhyme** because they end in the same sound.

Write two other words that rhyme.

_____

_____

Build Your Word List Reread the list of interesting words you noted on page 160. Choose a word and look up its definition. Write the word and the definition that best fits how the word is used in the poem in your writer's notebook.

Metaphor

A **metaphor** compares two very different things without using the words *like* or *as*. "His teeth are white pearls" is a metaphor. It compares teeth to pearls. It helps me visualize bright, white teeth.

FIND TEXT EVIDENCE

On page 160, I read that "Ginger's fingers are shooting stars." This is a metaphor. It compares Ginger's fingers to shooting stars. It helps me picture Ginger's fingers moving quickly.

Ginger's fingers are shooting stars,
They talk of adventurous trips to Mars.
Fingers talking without words,
Signing when sounds can't be heard.

Your Turn Reread "Ginger's Fingers" on page 160. Find another metaphor. What two things are compared? How does it help you visualize?

_____

_____

Diverse Images/Universal Images Group/Getty Images

Repetition and Rhyme

Repetition means that words or phrases in a poem are repeated. A **rhyme** is two or more words that end with the same sound, such as *pouring* and *roaring*.

FIND TEXT EVIDENCE

Reread "Captain's Log" on pages 162 and 163. Listen for words or phrases that are repeated. Think about why the poet uses repetition.

Page 162

Captain's Log,
May 12, 1868

We set sail from a port in Spain,
Sun high, no sign of rain.
The sea was satin, so blue—so blue.
Our ship was a bird, we flew—we flew.

Just past noon, how very weird,
Came a sound that we most feared.
Thunder rumbled, a giant drum.
Thunder rumbled, rum tum tum.

> **Quick Tip**
>
> Read poems aloud to listen for rhymes. Rhyming words do not have to be spelled alike to sound alike. Look at the spelling of *you* and *through*. These words look different, but reading them aloud reveals they have the same end sounds.

In the first stanza, the poet repeats the words so blue *and* we flew. *These words also rhyme. This repetition gives the poem a musical quality. It helps me feel the waves and how the ship moves on the sea.*

Your Turn Look at page 163 of "Captain's Log." Find two examples of repetition and two examples of rhyme. Write them here.

_____

_____

Narrative and Free Verse

Narrative poetry tells a story with a setting and characters. It often has stanzas, or groups of lines, that are the same length. It often rhymes.

Free Verse poetry doesn't always rhyme. It can have stanzas with different lengths. It can tell a story or just express a feeling.

FIND TEXT EVIDENCE

I can tell that "Captain's Log" is a narrative poem. It is a story of the ship's captain who inspires his crew during a bad storm.

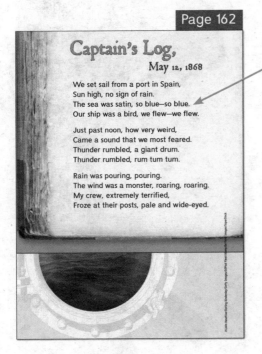

Page 162

Captain's Log,
May 12, 1868

We set sail from a port in Spain,
Sun high, no sign of rain.
The sea was satin, so blue—so blue.
Our ship was a bird, we flew—we flew.

Just past noon, how very weird,
Came a sound that we most feared.
Thunder rumbled, a giant drum.
Thunder rumbled, rum tum tum.

Rain was pouring, pouring.
The wind was a monster, roaring, roaring.
My crew, extremely terrified,
Froze at their posts, pale and wide-eyed.

"Captain's Log" is a narrative poem. It rhymes and has stanzas. It's set on a ship during a storm. This setting helps readers understand how characters feel and what they do.

COLLABORATE

Your Turn Reread "The Giant." Explain why it is a free verse poem. Write your answer below.

_____

_____

_____

Theme

The **theme** is the main message or lesson in a poem. A poem's topic is what it is about. Paraphrasing the details in a poem can help you figure out the theme.

🔍 FIND TEXT EVIDENCE

All the poems in this week are about inspirational people, but each poem has a different theme. I'll reread "The Giant" and look for details. I can use the details to paraphrase and figure out the theme.

> To paraphrase means to retell the meaning of something in your own words. Paraphrasing details will help you combine ideas to figure out the theme.

> **Detail**
>
> I sizzle when I dribble, and I'm lightning on the court.

↓

> **Detail**
>
> The other team might laugh to see a player so small.

↓

> **Theme**
>
> If you believe in yourself you can do anything.

Your Turn Reread "The Giant"on page 161. Paraphrase the details in your graphic organizer. Make sure they support the poem's theme.

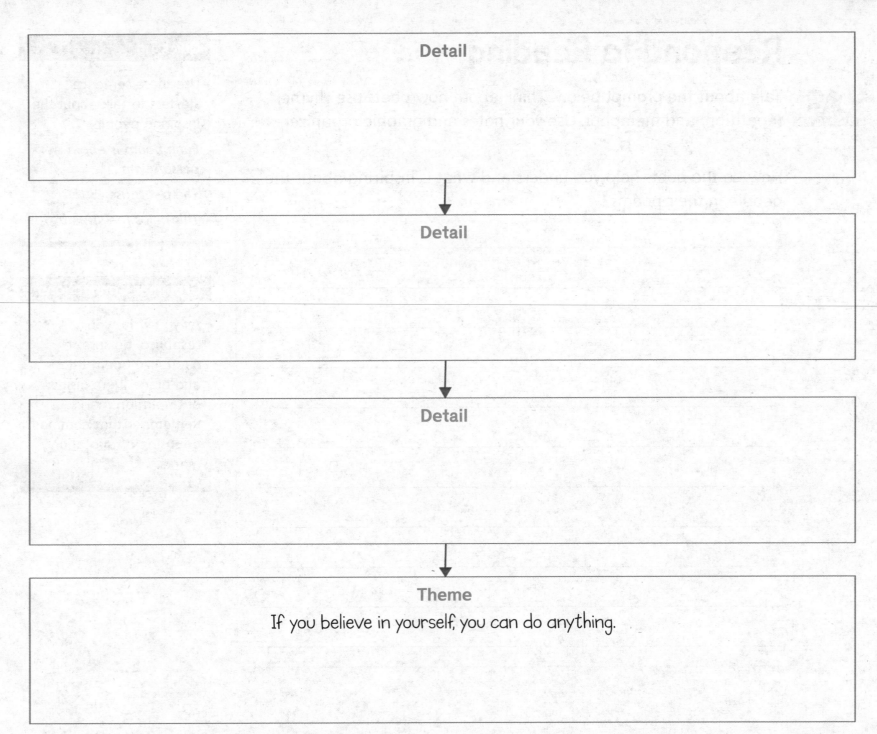

Detail

Detail

Detail

Theme

If you believe in yourself, you can do anything.

Respond to Reading

COLLABORATE

Talk about the prompt below. Think about how poets use rhyme, repetition, and metaphor. Use your notes and graphic organizer.

How do the poets help you understand what is inspiring about the people in their poems?

_____

_____

_____

_____

_____

_____

_____

_____

_____

Grammar Connections

As you write your response, be sure to capitalize poem titles and place them inside of quotation marks. Remember that commas go inside of quotation marks.

Primary and Secondary Sources

A **primary source** is information about a topic created by someone who experienced it. Examples include diary entries and letters. **Secondary sources** are created by someone who doesn't have firsthand knowledge of the topic. Examples include textbooks and encyclopedias.

Is the photograph below a primary or secondary source? Explain.

_____

What kind of information can you get from this photograph?

_____

Write an Acrostic Poem In an acrostic poem, the first letters of each line spell out a word or name. In this poem, the first letters of each line spell the word *cat*. Each line describes a cat.

> **C**uddly and cute
> **A**lways purring
> **T**ail swishes and swipes

Think of a person who inspires you. Then use these steps to write your own acrostic poem.

1. Write the name of the person in a vertical line on your paper.
2. Use primary and secondary sources to learn about the person. Tell a partner about the sources you used.
3. Use each letter of the person's name to write information about him or her. Then, add pictures to your poem.

> **Quick Tip**
>
> To figure out if something is a primary or secondary source, ask yourself: *Did the person who created this source see the event or know the person I'm researching?*

FatCamera/iStock/Getty Images

The Winningest Woman of the Iditarod Dog Sled Race

Literature Anthology: pages 320–321

 How does the poet help you understand how the narrator feels about finishing the Iditarod?

 Talk About It Reread page 321. Talk with a partner about what the Iditarod was like.

Cite Text Evidence What words and phrases show how the narrator feels about finishing the race? Write text evidence in the chart.

Evaluate Information

Notice that the second line and last line of the poem are the same. How does this repetition help express the narrator's point of view?

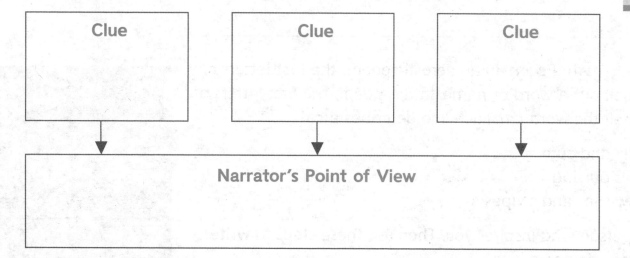

Clue	Clue	Clue

Narrator's Point of View

Write The poet helps me understand how the narrator feels by

_____

_____

The Brave Ones

? How does the poet's use of repetition in "The Brave Ones" help you visualize what it is like to fight a fire?

Talk About It Reread page 322. Talk with a partner about how the poet's words and phrases make you feel.

Cite Text Evidence What words and phrases does the poet repeat? Write them in the chart.

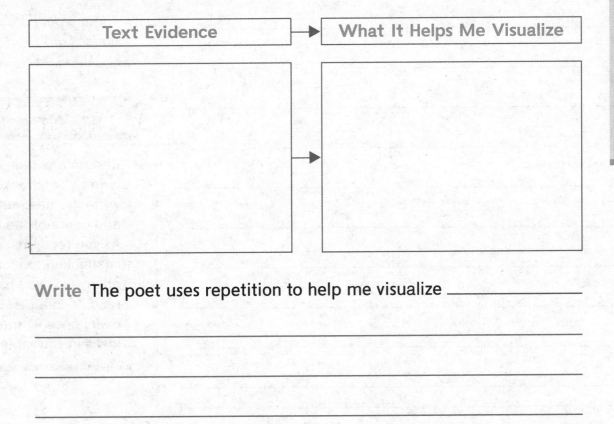

Text Evidence	→	What It Helps Me Visualize

Write The poet uses repetition to help me visualize _____

_____

_____

_____

Respond to Reading

Answer the prompt below. Think about how poets use repetition in their poems. Use your notes and graphic organizer.

How do the poets use repetition to help you understand the message in their poems?

_____

_____

_____

_____

_____

_____

_____

_____

_____

_____

 How does the poet use words and phrases to help you visualize what Narcissa is doing?

 Talk About It Reread the first and second stanzas on page 325. Turn and talk with a partner about what Narcissa is doing.

Literature Anthology: pages 324–325

Cite Text Evidence What clues in the first and second stanzas help you picture what Narcissa is doing? Write text evidence in the chart.

Quick Tip

A verb is a word that shows action. Look for verbs to help yourself visualize what characters are doing.

Clue	Clue	Clue

↓   ↓   ↓

What I Visualize

Write I can visualize what Narcissa is doing because _____

_____

_____

_____

_____

? **Why does the poet repeat the word *still* at the end of the poem?**

Talk About It Reread the third and fourth stanzas on page 325. Talk with a partner about what Narcissa is doing and how she is changing.

Cite Text Evidence What clues help you understand why the poet repeats the word *still*? Write text evidence in the chart.

Text Evidence	What It Shows

Write The author repeats the word *still* to _____

_____

_____

Imagery

Poets choose words and phrases that help you visualize, or picture in your mind, what is happening in a poem. This is called **imagery**.

🔍 FIND TEXT EVIDENCE

*On page 325 in the third stanza of "Narcissa" in the **Literature Anthology**, the poet writes that Narcissa looks like an ancient queen, "in pomp and purple veil." This description helps me picture Narcissa sitting tall on her throne with a purple veil draped over her head.*

Your Turn Reread the first stanza of "Narcissa" on page 325.

- How does the poet help you visualize what Narcissa is doing?

_____

_____

_____

- How does this help you understand how Narcissa is feeling?

_____

_____

_____

As you write, use descriptions of how things look, sound, smell, and feel to help your readers picture what is happening and what characters are experiencing.

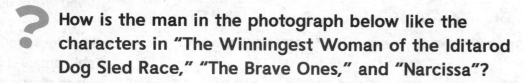

Text Connections

? **How is the man in the photograph below like the characters in "The Winningest Woman of the Iditarod Dog Sled Race," "The Brave Ones," and "Narcissa"?**

Talk About It Look at the photograph and read the caption. Discuss what the grandfather and his grandson are doing.

Cite Text Evidence **Circle** details in the photograph that help you understand what each person is doing. **Underline** evidence in the caption that gives you more information about what is going on.

Write The grandfather and the characters in the poems are alike

because they _____

_____

_____

_____

_____

_____

_____

Alex is a gardener. He works in a community garden on the weekends. He loves to take his grandson with him to show him how to grow vegetables and flowers.

Expression

Think about how the words of a poem make you feel as you read them. Reading a poem with **expression** makes the poem more interesting for listeners and helps them understand its topic, or what the poem is about.

Page 163

I grabbed a rope, reached for the mast,
And got back to the helm at last—at last
Shook off the rain, looked at my crew,
"Steady lads, I'll get us through."

I feel afraid as the captain grabs for the rope and relieved when he gets back to the helm. I feel proud when I read what he tells his crew. I can use my voice to show how I feel as I read.

Your Turn Take turns reading "Captain's Log" on pages 162 and 163 aloud with a partner. Visualize what is happening in the poem. What do the characters feel? Express these feelings as you read.

Afterward think about how you did. Complete these sentences.

I remembered to _____

_____

Next time I will _____

_____

Literature Anthology:
pages 320–321

Expert Model

Features of a Narrative Poem

A **narrative poem** is a kind of poem. A narrative poem

- tells a story with characters and a setting
- often has stanzas, or groups of lines
- often rhymes

Analyze an Expert Model A good way to learn how to write a narrative poem is to study one. Reread the second stanza of "The Winningest Woman of the Iditarod Dog Sled Race" on page 321 of the **Literature Anthology**. Use text evidence and write your answers below.

How does the poet help you visualize what moose are like

on the trail? _____

_____

_____

How do you know how the narrator feels about the Iditarod race?

_____

_____

Word Wise

The poet's repetition of the phrase "I did" echoes the sound of the word *Iditarod*. This helps readers draw a connection between the Iditarod dog sled race and the narrator's feelings about it.

Plan: Choose Your Topic

COLLABORATE

Brainstorm With a partner, make a list of people who are inspiring. Talk about what those people did and why they are inspiring. Use the sentence starters below to discuss your ideas.

One person who did something inspiring is . . .

I am inspired because . . .

Writing Prompt Choose one of the people you talked about. Write a narrative poem about what the person did.

I will write about _____

Purpose and Audience Some poems are written to express a feeling or emotion. Others tell a story or express an idea. Poems are often written to entertain the reader. I am writing this poem to

_____

_____

Now think about your audience. Who will read your poem?

My audience will be _____

Freewrite Think about the person you chose and why he or she inspires you. Write everything you know about this person in your writer's notebook. Keep writing until your teacher tells you to stop.

Plan: Ideas

Quick Tip

The poet of "The Winningest Woman of the Iditarod" uses the phrase "freeze the whiskers in a beard" to help readers picture how cold it is during the race.

Ideas Poets choose words and phrases that bring their ideas to life and help readers form pictures in their minds. These words and phrases might describe how something looks, tastes, smells, or feels.

Think about the inspiring person you are writing your poem about. Use your freewrite to choose important ideas to include in your poem. Write those ideas here.

_____

_____

_____

_____

_____

_____

_____

Plan Draw an Idea web in your writer's notebook. In the center circle, write the name of the person your poem is about. Then, add ideas, words and phrases to your Idea web.

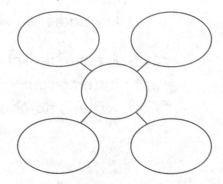

Draft

Repetition and Rhyme Poems are often organized into stanzas and may use repetition and rhyme. In this stanza from "Captain's Log, May 12, 1868," the poet repeats words to help you visualize what is happening and uses rhyme to give the poem a musical quality.

> A huge wave lifted up our ship.
>
> My feet began to slip, slip, slip.
>
> I knew that it was up to me,
>
> To guide us through that stormy sea.

Use the above stanza as a model to write a stanza about one of the ideas from your idea web. Try to use both repetition and rhyme.

_____

_____

_____

_____

_____

Write a Draft Look over your freewrite and word web. Use them to complete your poem by writing stanzas about your other ideas. Make sure your poem shows why the person you chose is inspiring.

Revise

Figurative Language Poets often use figurative language, such as similes and metaphors, to compare two things. A simile compares two things using the words *like* or *as*. A metaphor compares two things without using *like* or *as*. Using figurative language helps readers visualize, or picture, what you are describing.

Reread "The Giant" on page 161. Talk with a partner about how the poet compares things. Find three things the poet compares the basketball player to. Write them here.

_____

_____

_____

Revise It's time to revise your writing. Read your draft and look for places where you might

- use precise nouns, strong verbs, or colorful adjectives

- use figurative language

Circle two phrases in your draft that you can change. Revise and write them here.

1 _____

2 _____

Quick Tip

In a poem, every word counts! As you revise, make sure you choose words and phrases that help tell the story and help your readers visualize your ideas.

Peer Conferences

Review a Draft Listen carefully as a partner reads his or her draft aloud. Say what you like about the draft. Use these sentence starters to discuss your partner's draft.

I like this part of the poem because . . .

Add a more colorful adjective or strong verb to . . .

Try using figurative language here to describe . . .

I have a question about . . .

Partner Feedback After you take turns giving each other feedback, write one of the suggestions from your partner that you will use in your revision.

_____

_____

_____

Revision After you finish your peer conference, use the Revising Checklist to figure out what you can change to make your poem better. Remember to use the rubric on page 187 to help with your revision.

✓ Revising Checklist

☐ Are my ideas clear?

☐ Did I use repetition to focus on important words or phrases?

☐ Is my word choice strong and descriptive?

☐ Did I use figurative language to make my poem more interesting?

Edit and Proofread

After you revise your narrative poem, proofread it to find any mistakes in grammar, spelling, and punctuation. Read your draft at least three times. This will help you catch any mistakes. Use the checklist below to edit your sentences.

✔ Editing Checklist

- ☐ Is the first word of each line capitalized?
- ☐ Are names and other proper nouns capitalized?
- ☐ Do the lines have the correct punctuation?
- ☐ Are all words spelled correctly?

List two mistakes that you found as you proofread your poem.

1 _____

_____

_____

2 _____

_____

_____

 Tech Tip

If you wrote your draft on a computer, use the spell-check feature to find spelling mistakes. The spell-check tool can be especially helpful for correctly spelling irregular verbs.

Grammar Connections

When you proofread your draft, remember that some of your verbs might be irregular. In the past tense, irregular verbs do not follow regular spelling rules. For example, the past tense of the irregular verb *ride* is *rode*.

Publish, Present, and Evaluate

Publishing When you publish your writing, you create a neat final copy that is free of mistakes. If you are not using a computer, use your best handwriting. Write legibly in print or cursive.

Presentation Before you are ready to present, practice your presentation. Use the presenting checklist.

Evaluate After you publish your poem, use the rubric to evaluate it.

What did you do successfully? _____

_____

What needs more work? _____

_____

✔ **Presenting Checklist**

☐ Look at your audience.

☐ Speak loudly and clearly.

☐ Read with expression to show the challenge that was overcome.

☐ Pause at the end of lines or phrases.

4	3	2	1
• very clearly tells a story and expresses feelings • excellent use of figurative language • excellent word choice • very few spelling, grammar, or punctuation errors	• clearly tells a story and expresses feelings • good use of figurative language • good word choice • some spelling, grammar, or punctuation errors	• tells a story or expresses feelings • not enough figurative language • word choice could be more precise • several spelling, grammar, and punctuation errors	• the story or feelings are unclear • no figurative language • uses common words • many spelling, grammar, and punctuation errors

SHOW WHAT YOU LEARNED

Spiral Review

You have learned new skills and strategies in Unit 4 that will help you read more critically. Now it is time to practice what you have learned.

- Sentence Clues
- Reread
- Compare and Contrast
- Author's Message
- Prefixes
- Ask and Answer Questions
- Point of View
- Theme

Connect to Content

- Write a Journal Entry
- Select a Genre
- Read Digitally

Read the selection and choose the best answer to each question.

Armadillo: Little Armored One

[1] When you think of Texas wildlife, you probably picture an armadillo. In 1995, the nine-banded armadillo became the state's official small mammal. Today, this odd-looking creature has its picture on everything from T-shirts to postcards! There are twenty different kinds of armadillos. However, the nine-banded armadillo is the only one found in Texas. Like all animals, armadillos have adapted, or changed, to survive in their environment.

Protection

[2] Armadillos are part of the same animal family as sloths and anteaters. Like these animals, armadillos usually move slowly. However, they can run up to 30 miles per hour to escape from coyotes and other predators that want to eat them. They're also protected by an unusual feature.

[3] The name *armadillo* comes from a Spanish word that means "little armored one." The armadillo's "armor" is made of bony plates that cover its back, legs, head, and tail. These bony plates are like a turtle's shell. Turtles, however, are reptiles. Armadillos are the only mammals that have this kind of bony armor.

Finding Food

[4]   Like sloths and anteaters, armadillos sleep a lot and eat insects. During the summer, they hunt at night to keep cool. Long hairs on the sides of their bellies help them feel around in the dark. They also have a good sense of smell. They search the ground for ants, beetles, and termites. They sniff and snort like a pig.

[5]   Armadillos have strong legs and huge front claws that make them very good diggers. Like anteaters and sloths, they have long, sticky tongues. This helps them reach ants, termites, and other insects that live in tunnels.

[6]   The armadillo might look strange, but its odd adaptations have helped this Texas favorite survive!

SHOW WHAT YOU LEARNED

1 Reread paragraph 1. Which kinds of armadillos live in Texas?

   A The three-banded armadillo

   B The five-banded armadillo

   C The nine-banded armadillo

   D All of the above

Quick Tip

Rereading can help you better understand something you might not have understood during your first reading.

2 In paragraph 2, what clue tells you the meaning of *predator*?

   F Sloths and anteaters

   G Want to eat them

   H Coyote

   J Both G and H

3 According to the passage, what is one way that anteaters, sloths, and armadillos are alike?

   A They live in Texas.

   B They are eaten by coyotes.

   C They move slowly.

   D They are odd looking.

4 Which sentence best describes the author's message?

   F Armadillos have adapted, or changed, to survive in their environment.

   G Armadillos belong to a group of animals that includes sloths and anteaters.

   H Armadillos are very popular in Texas.

   J Armadillos are strange-looking animals.

Read the selection and choose the best answer to each question.

Change *for* OCELOTS

[1] "What can we do to help the ocelots?" Miguel asked.

[2] Miguel's class was studying Texas wildlife. They had just learned that the ocelot was in danger of extinction. Miguel's teacher, Mr. Clark, explained that only between 80 and 120 of these small wildcats still lived in Texas. Soon there could be none.

[3] "Ocelots are found only in South Texas," Mr. Clark said. "Their numbers are dropping, and their future is uncertain. The main danger is highways. Many cats are killed by cars."

[4] "There are animal groups that help ocelots and other animals survive, but they need help," Mr. Clark said. "One way we can help is to raise money."

[5] Mr. Clark showed the students a website. The website explained that for 35 dollars, people could "adopt" an ocelot. "I thought we could raise money to do it," he said.

[6] "Would the ocelot stay in our classroom?" Piper asked.

SHOW WHAT YOU LEARNED

7   "We wouldn't really adopt an ocelot," Mr. Clark explained. "We would donate money to help save it. In return, we would get pictures, a fact sheet, and a certificate to show that we care about what happens to these beautiful cats."

8   "I want to do it," said Miguel. The rest of the class agreed.

9   "How can we raise the money?" asked Mr. Clark. The class came up with different ideas. One boy suggested a bake sale. One girl suggested a lemonade stand. Another wanted to have a garage sale.

10   "I have a lot of change at home," said Miguel. "I could donate it." Several other students said they had change, too. They agreed that a change drive was a good idea.

11   The following Friday, the class counted the change they had raised. They had $68.95.

12   "Since we're so close to $70, I'm going to give the rest so we can adopt two ocelots!" Mr. Clark exclaimed. The whole class cheered and clapped.

13   "It's amazing what we can do when we care enough to work together," said Miguel.

1 Which word in paragraph 3 contains a prefix?

A explained

B dropping

C uncertain

D highways

2 How did Mr. Clark's class raise money to help the ocelots?

F They had a bake sale.

G They had a lemonade stand.

H They had a change drive.

J They had a garage sale.

3 Why does Miguel want to help ocelots?

A They are found in Texas.

B Their numbers are dropping.

C He has a lot of change at home.

D He wants to raise money.

4 In which paragraph does the author share the theme of the story?

F 2

G 3

H 11

J 13

> **Quick Tip**
>
> The theme is the message, or lesson, the author would like readers to learn from the story.

EXTEND YOUR LEARNING

COMPARING GENRES

COLLABORATE

- In the **Literature Anthology,** reread the realistic fiction story *Clementine and the Family Meeting* on pages 298–303 and the narrative poem "The Winningest Woman of the Iditarod Dog Sled Race" on pages 320–321.

- Use the Venn diagram below to show how the two genres are the same and different.

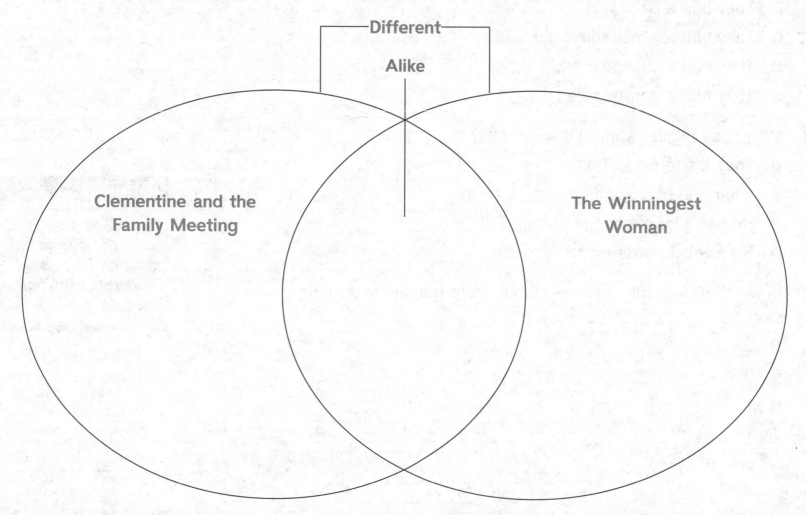

Different

Alike

Clementine and the Family Meeting

The Winningest Woman

MAIN IDEA AND KEY DETAILS

COLLABORATE

The main idea is the most important point the author makes about a topic. Key details tell about the main idea.

• Read the passage below.

• Paraphrase important details in the graphic organizer.

• Figure out what the details have in common to find the main idea.

   NASA is part of the U.S. government. NASA stands for National Aeronautics and Space Administration. NASA was started to explore space. In 1969, NASA's Apollo 11 mission put the first person on the Moon. NASA continues to explore space today.

Detail
Detail
Detail
Main Idea

EXTEND YOUR LEARNING

WRITE A JOURNAL ENTRY

People use a journal to record their thoughts and opinions. A journal can also include facts that you learn and want to remember.

- Read about someone who met a goal or a challenge.

- Write a journal entry from the person's point of view.

- Write what the person did to meet the goal or challenge.

The person in my journal entry is _____

I chose this person because _____

SELECT A GENRE

Animals survive by adapting to where they live. Choose two animals that live in the same environment.

- Research the two animals you chose. Generate questions. How does this animal survive? Does this animal have a special feature?

- Choose a genre for presenting your research. When choosing your genre, think about your audience. For example, you could write an expository essay, a persuasive essay, or a poem. Then plan your draft by freewriting, brainstorming, or mapping your ideas in an Idea web. Edit your work and present it to an audience.

Something I learned while working on this presentation is _____

_____

_____

FORBIDDEN FOODS

Log on to **my.mheducation.com** and read the Time for Kids online article "Forbidden Foods," including the information found in the interactive elements. Answer the questions below.

Time for Kids: "Forbidden Foods"

- How is the Top 5 Most Common Food Allergies interactive feature helpful?

_____

- Why does the author include a link to kidshealth.org?

_____

- After you click on kidshealth.org, enter "food allergies" in the search box. Then choose a food allergy topic to click on.

Which food allergy did you click on? _____

Write something you learned about that food allergy. _____

_____

_____

_____

_____

Hurst/Alamy;(b)Viktor Kunz/Shutterstock

WHAT DID YOU LEARN?

Use the rubric to evaluate yourself on the skills that you learned in this unit. Write your scores in the boxes below.

4	3	2	1
I can successfully identify all examples of this skill.	I can identify most examples of this skill.	I can identify a few examples of this skill.	I need to work on this skill more.

☐ Point of View

☐ Prefixes

☐ Compare/Contrast

☐ Sentence Clues

☐ Theme

☐ Metaphors

Something I need to work more on is _____ because

_____

_____

_____

Text-to-Self Think back over the texts that you have read in this unit. Choose one text and write a short paragraph explaining a personal connection that you have made to the text.

I made a personal connection to _____

because _____

_____

Present Your Work

COLLABORATE

Discuss how you will present your acrostic poem to the class. Use the Presenting Checklist as you practice your presentation. Discuss the sentence starters below and write your answers.

Quick Tip

Before you present your poem, practice reading it with expression. Know your poem well enough that you can look at your audience as you read it.

An interesting fact I learned about the person or event is _____

_____

_____

I would like to know more about _____

_____

_____

_____

Presenting Checklist

☐ I will practice reading my poem out loud.

☐ I will read so that each line is clear.

☐ I will speak loudly enough for all to hear.

☐ I will use my voice to add expression to my poem.